THE VOICE THAT MEANS BUSINESS

HOW TO SPEAK WITH AUTHORITY, CONFIDENCE AND CREDIBILITY ANYTIME, ANYWHERE

LINDA B. SHIELDS, M.S., CCC-SLP

Liberty Publishing Group
Egg Harbor • Frederick • Raleigh

Library of Congress Cataloging-in-Publication Data.
    Shields, Linda, 1948-
    The Voice That Means Business
    p.cm.
    Includes bibliographical references
    ISBN 1-893095-11-8

    1. Management 2. Communications
    3. Career   4. Business

    10 9 8 7 6 5 4 3 2 1

Dedication

This book is dedicated to my precious mother, Mary Franke Lazar Hardy. She is more than my Mom. She is my Hero. I admire her strength,courage and determination in the face of enormous obstacles. Mom has dedicated her life to caring for others. A true Angel of compassion, Mary has healed the bodies and spirits of countless hurting souls.

I acknowledge Mom for nursing me through critical illness, paralyz-ing shyness and extreme emotional pain and loss. I thank her for rubbing my back, singing "God Will Take Care of You" and putting up with my rebellion once I finally found my "voice."

I rejoice in the fact that she delights in my work, contributes articles for my business and cheers me on when I get weary. I especially appreciate her contribution to my visual appearance ... .the joyful shopping expedi-tions have enhanced my platform image immensely!

I love you unconditionally Mary Franke Lazar Hardy. I could never have had the courage to do what I so adore doing without you. Thanks for reminding me to stand up straight and proud as I fulfill God's purpose for my life. You have certainly fulfilled yours ... and continue to do so.

Note from the author, Second Printing:

Mary passed away peacefully on July 9, 2003. Her last comment about this book was: "It's really a good read, Linda Marie!" That was quite an endorsement from a tough critic.

Contents

Part III: The Vocal You

Part IV: The Verbal You

INTRODUCTION

People have got to get on speaking terms with themselves. Most people spend a fortune on their hair, skin, nails, body and clothing, but neglect the one feature that can make or break their career – their voice. Madison Avenue warns us constantly about offensive personal characteristics such as bad breath, body odor and tar-stained teeth. We take immediate steps to avoid these "anti-social" impressions, but fail miserably when it comes to fine-tuning our rich and powerful vocal instrument.

Do your best friends tell you about your less-than-adequate speaking habits? Do they complain about your weak, namby-pamby voice? Have they criticized your faulty diction or questioned your improper grammar? Does your voice sound nasal or whiny, hoarse or raspy, tense or shrill, authoritative or wimpy?

In today's economy, everyone has to become a master of powerful communication skills or they'll be lost in the shuffle. The trouble is, while many of us can occasionally "amp up" our vocal authority, it's not something we do easily – or consistently. All too often, because of past habits of speaking and acting, we can unconsciously sabotage the very message of confidence and control we want to project.

I can attribute my speaking, consulting and coaching career to an event that happened early in my life. When I was four years old, my father died, and I stopped speaking. For one solid year, I never uttered a single word to anyone – if I couldn't talk to him, I didn't want to talk to anybody. To this day, my mother can't believe what I do for a living because she absolutely despaired of my ever saying another word.

It was only through the loving attention of my kindergarten teacher that one day I began using my voice again. Then, through the coaching of many wonderful mentors over the years (plus a lot of soul-searching on my part), I "evolved" into my life calling. I earned B.S. and M.S. degrees in speech pathology and began my career as a speech pathologist in a little farming community near Ann Arbor, Michigan. I saw children with speech and voice problems ranging from mild lisps to incomprehensible stutters. I worked with children as young as eight or nine who already had nodes on their vocal cords because they had misused their voices from the time they started speaking. Untreated, these children would have lost their voices entirely or needed to have the nodes surgically removed. Luckily, with some diligent speech training, they learned how to speak in their natural, unforced voices and the nodes miraculously disappeared.

After a while, I shifted gears and taught drama in Ohio, Pennsylvania and North Carolina. It was great fun, and I learned even more about the power of vocal image as I helped many high school students eliminate Southern drawls or cultivate a British accent for a school play. But as I taught children, I also listened to parents whose regional accents and poor grammar held them back from gaining the promotions they deserved. I spoke to business people who were too frightened to deliver a prepared speech in public. And I met far too many professional women with resumés that shouted, "I know what I'm doing," but whose little-girl voices and gestures whimpered, "Please take care of me."

So I began coaching business people to help them develop the vocal, visual and verbal image that others would recognize as being "good for business." I called my company "Speaking with Authority, Inc." because I felt I could speak with authority on this subject. I wanted to help people discover and use their own personal, authoritative, memorable style of speech and communication.

As I became more and more successful as a speaker and consultant, someone told me about a marvelous group called the National Speakers Association (NSA). "Linda," this person said, "These are the people who need you the most, because they absolutely have to speak with authority!" Through the years, I not only have helped hundreds of NSA members eliminate vocal habits that might have shortened their careers, but I also have developed a reputation as NSA's unofficial voice coach.

One of the reasons I love my work is that in addition to working with professional speakers, I coach men and women on the corporate "front lines." These "invisible" and under-acknowledged folks include reservation agents at major hotel chains like Holiday Inn and Marriott, information operators at Sprint, stockbrokers and sales people who spend their entire business day on the phone, and teachers (God bless 'em!) who guide the developing minds of our children. (Weren't your favorite teachers the ones who made learning come alive through stories?) Teachers need good story-telling voices. Their voices are their livelihoods. Unfortunately, many of my clients, including teachers, have abused and misused their voices before they come to me. It's a joy to know that the training I provide not only saves their voices from serious damage, but also makes their voices "vocal friendly" for guests, customers, clients, colleagues and students.

I believe it is possible for everyone in business today to speak with authority, confidence and credibility – anytime, anywhere.

This book is not a vocal charm school manual – it serves a much higher purpose than teaching people how to sound pretty and move gracefully! *The Voice that Means Business* shows how you can...

✔ have the voice, image, and facility with language that will move you ahead of "voice-challenged" colleagues;

✔ use the highest capabilities of your physical and vocal instruments to communicate your message effectively, credibly; and

✔ speak with authority in any situation – with your boss, your employees, your audience, your local government, your family – and achieve more personal and professional success as a result.

If you approach the exercises in this book with a spirit of fun, adventure and willingness to look silly sometimes (at least in the privacy of your own home or office), you'll speak with more authority, confidence and credibility than you could have imagined.

After all, two of the secrets of speaking with authority are flexibility and fun. Take a cue from a group of U.S. Army protocol officers – a pretty dignified bunch – who, under my guidance, agreed to pinch their noses and talk to each other sounding like Lily Tomlin's "Edith Ann" character. They even moved around the room imitating the walks of lions or elephants during one of the "expressive" exercises. If they can do it (and get results) you can, too!

So let's get started. Whether you're a business executive who wants to pick up a few pointers on how to come across better in meetings, a sales manager who wants to give a successful presentation at your next industry convention,or a stockbroker, hotel operator, teacher or anyone else whose livelihood depends upon the quality of their voice...you will find immense value in this book.

I'm delighted to be your vocal awareness guide. I hope you will find your journey exciting as you begin to speak with authority, confidence and grace. All it takes is a little awareness, patience and commitment. I guarantee you will see results. There's no limit to the transformation that you can experience.

Take advantage of the hints and shortcuts in this book and your speaking voice will become clear, colorful, and captivating. People will listen when you speak. Don't wait until an emergency arises: when you are about to be interviewed for a promotion or new job, meet with a prospective client, discuss a subordinate's performance appraisal, or deliver a technical presentation.

The time to start is now. Read the following pages with care. Enjoy the exercises. Take each recommendation to heart. Don't skip anything. The part you over-look may be the very piece you need most. This book can dramatically improve your speaking competence and change your life.

PART ONE

WHY YOUR CAREER DEPENDS ON THIS BOOK

In talking with successful (people) in large companies, I hear one recurrent theme: the willingness to pay the price. This phrase implies an intense motivation, a burning desire to become...successful.

(Thomas R. Horton, President and CEO, AMA)

CHAPTER ONE

IS YOUR VOICE AN ASSET OR LIABILITY?

Let thy speech be better than silence; or be silent. (Dionysius)

Your resumé may be your "calling card," but your voice is your "business card." Whether you like it or not, people who articulate well – over the phone, in front of a group or face-to-face – are generally perceived to be more intelligent, professional, and successful than someone who possesses average communication skills. Your voice is not a neutral characteristic, skill or trait. It can literally make or break your career. It's either a wonderful asset or an embarrassing, if not serious, professional liability.

The quality of your voice very definitely affects the quality of your career. You don't have to "own" a voice as distinctive and cultured as James Earl Jones' phenomenal voice, or Paul Harvey's widely-recognized celebrity voice; but your voice must meet muster. You must be able to carry just the right amount of inflection, a certain timbre, rhythm and legibility. Your intonation and range must vary. Your gestures and facial expressions must complement your message. All of your verbal, vocal and visual cues must match. You must have *the voice that means business, makes business and keeps business* to remain competitive in today's highly specialized marketplace.

> The object of oratory is not truth, but persuasion.
> (*Thomas Macaulay*)

A LESSON FROM HOLLYWOOD

Too many people take a good speaking voice for granted. To be able to articulate clearly and concisely, confidently and credibly, is an essential part of anyone's communication repertoire. There was a time when actions spoke louder than words. The silent movies of the early 1900's made stars out of actors who looked good and moved well. When sound movies arrived in the late 1920's, a whole generation of motion picture actors lost their competitive edge to newcomers who sounded as good as they looked.

Before "talkies" there had been no need for the stars of silent film to speak well. After all, their adoring fans could not hear them. Sound caught these cinematic dinosaurs speechless and unprepared. One promising star, after hearing her recorded voice for the first time, overdosed on sleeping pills. Corinne Griffith, dream girl of the silent films, retired immediately upon hearing a critic's unkind comment: "Pretty Corinne Griffith talks through her nose."

A few months before sound tracks were added to motion pictures. John Gilbert, successor to Rudolph Valentino as the next Casanova of the silver screen, signed a four-year contract worth a million dollars a year. In his first picture under the new "talkie" format, Gilbert's thin, reedy, tenor voice prompted snickers of derision from the same moviegoers who had cheered his passionate, theatrical antics less than a year before. The *ear* movie had canceled the *eye* movie and brought many a promising career to a screeching halt.

The make-or-break affects of vocal, verbal and visual variety apply to every profession and not just the movie industry. There's no doubt about it, being able to speak effectively – anywhere, anytime – is vitally important and will help accelerate your career sooner than later if you have that "something"…that special speaking quality that helps you stand out…that distinctive ability to speak with authority, confidence and credibility in any situation.

Your voice can be a career stopper – or a career starter. Whether you are trying to close a million-dollar deal with a client… explaining to an employer why you deserve that promotion and raise…or warning your children to cruise the internet responsibly, you'd better be able to speak with authority, confidence and credibility.

It doesn't matter if you are a manager, staff member, technician, custodian or CEO, your voice is one of the critical business communication tools which determines how people respond to you and treat you. A squeaky, soft voice tends to undermine your credibility. A high-pitched, searing voice is tough on the ears and patience. A rich, low voice tends to retail confidence and trustworthiness.

Good speaking skills and a dynamic voice don't come automatically for most people. Like any other self-development skill, vocal competence and verbal confidence take time to develop. You can polish your voice just as you polish an upcoming speech or fine tune a project report. All it takes is awareness and practice.

I believe you may be one of those rare individuals who wants to improve your vocal, verbal and visual image.

Otherwise, you wouldn't have invested you time and money in this book. The good news is I have no doubt that you can speak with authority, confidence and credibility. You can if you think you can and this book can show you how.

Because I have spent the last fifteen years working with professional speakers, business people, politicians, performers, telephone operators and protocol officers, I can say (with authority!) that everyone has his or her own style and approach to communicating powerfully and authentically. Through this book, you will learn to use your own voice, mind and body to speak with authority.

> *Eloquence is the power to translate a truth into language perfectly intelligible to the person to whom you speak.*
> *(Ralph Waldo Emerson, essayist & poet)*

THE 'OMIGOSH' EXPERIENCE

In a business world filled with answering machines, voice mail, transcribers and video conferencing equipment, at one time or another we've all had what I call the 'omigosh' experience – we see or hear ourselves recorded and think, "Oh, my gosh, is that really what I sound or look like?" And usually, 'omigosh' is followed by *blecch* or *yuk* or some other expression of disgust.

You realize that how you *think* you sound and how you *actually* sound are quite different. The *you* you thought you were and the *you* you saw or heard on the recording device may have seemed like two entirely different people. Most of us become very self-conscious when we are "caught" on camera or "captured" on tape. 'Omigosh' experiences are due to one of two reasons:

1. You weren't aware of the effects of some of your speaking habits and body language;
2. You felt stressed by unfamiliar circumstances – speaking to a large group, a confrontation with a co-worker, being interviewed on camera, etc.

Janet, a radio account executive, had a 'omigosh' experience when the station told her to "do something" about her voice mail messages. Janet was shocked and confused. She thought her enthusiastic, rapid-fire approach to marketing calls was perfect for the station's rock format. When she asked the station manager to explain, he said, "Your voice sounds like a machine gun – loud and fast. So...do something! You've got to slow down!"

When she contacted my office, I had to replay the message several times just to get the phone number, and hold the receiver away from my ear because of her loud voice. Her manager was right. Potential sales and revenue were being lost whenever she spoke. When I played her voice mail message in my office, Janet said – you guessed it – "Oh my gosh! Is that really me? I sound awful." Until that moment she was unaware that her loud, rapid fire speaking voice projected the image of an aggressive salesperson who seemed desperate and unsure of herself. Sound familiar?

Let me give you a few more examples of 'omigosh' experiences I've seen in my fifteen-year career of teaching others to speak with authority:

- An executive assistant in a real estate company was constantly being propositioned by clients over the phone. She couldn't figure out what the problem was – she always dressed and acted in a professional manner. Finally, someone told her, "Jane, when you talk to people you sound just like Marilyn Monroe. No wonder the guys on the phone think you are interested in more than just a real estate listing!" Jane's breathy, soft voice was undermining her efforts to speak with authority, confidence and credibility.

- An engineer friend of mine was promoted to head a division of the computer company where he had been employed for several years. His new responsibilities included making presentations to clients about the division's computer net-working capabilities. After his first presentation, the company sales manager went to the CEO and said, "If you want us to make sales, never send Tom with me again. He was so boring he put half the room to sleep!"

Tom had spent all his working life at a desk dealing with numbers. He had no idea how to talk about computers so lay-people could understand. He reeled off statistics and parameters and specifications in a flat, monotone voice that was almost inaudible to anyone three feet away. On top of that, Tom didn't dress for success. He wore his usual workday "uniform," a short-sleeved white shirt, blue pants, tie and unshined shoes – which paled in comparison to the sales manager's handsome suit and immaculate appearance.

Did Tom know more than anyone else about the computer networking capabilities offered by his company? Absolutely! Was he effective in communicating this to the client? Not in the least. To carry out the responsibilities of his new position, will Tom have to make a few changes so he can speak with authority? According to Tom's CEO, he'd better!

These people undermined their own attempts to speak with authority. Luckily, developing a "good for business" communication style only requires three things: awareness, commitment and practice. I'm happy to report that these people handled their communication dilemmas. They overcame all kinds of barriers and successfully developed their ability to speak with confidence and control. Some of their changes were nothing short of miraculous!

> *The exact words that you use are far less important than the energy, intensity and conviction with which you use them.*
> *(Jules Rose, V.P. Sloan Supermarkets)*

WHAT'S YOUR AUTHORITY QUOTIENT?

Speaking with authority is "the ability to consistently use your voice, your words, and your body language to communicate with strength, power and clarity." When you speak with authority, you project an image of believability, conviction and integrity. You send the message, "I am someone you can trust, someone you will want to do business with." People will give you their confidence and respect when you come across as someone who is credible and in control.

How would you rate your current ability to speak with authority, confidence and credibility? Do you have a voice that means business, makes business and keeps business? Are you ready to assess your Authority Quotient? If so, you will need a small tape recorder and a microphone. Find a quiet place where you will not be interrupted for at least half an hour. Complete the following exercises:

ASSIGNMENT #1:

The situation – Imagine you are calling someone important with whom you have a business relationship. It could be your boss, a company CEO, an important client (or someone who could be an important client in the future), the head of another department in your company, etc. You speak to a secretary who puts you through to this person's voice mail. You have 45 seconds to leave a message that will get your point across and compel this person to call you back.

Your Assignment – Create your 45-second message and then record it on the tape recorder. You can practice what you're going to say as often as you wish, but you will have only one opportunity to record your message. Time yourself (or have a friend time you) to make sure you don't run over the allotted time.

ASSIGNMENT #2:

The situation – Imagine you have a teenage child or friend whom you care deeply about. You find out this teenager is doing something that worries you very much – he or she is hanging around with the wrong crowd, or is flunking a subject in school, or is engaging in careless behavior concerning sex, drugs, cigarettes, and so on. You call to confront the teen, and you get the answering machine. You need to leave a message that expresses your concern and love and will ensure that the teen will call you back.

Your Assignment – Create your message and then record it following the recording from Assignment #1. Once again, you may rehearse as much as you like, but you only have one opportunity to record it. There is no time limit on this message, but you should time yourself to see how long you speak.

ASSIGNMENT #3:

The situation – You have to record a new greeting for your own answering machine or voice mail. The greeting can be no more than 30 seconds long, and should be appropriate for the context (either your voice mail at work, or your answering machine at home).

Your Assignment – Create your new greeting and record it. Make sure you don't erase the previous two assignments, and time yourself so your message is no more than 30 seconds long.

ASSIGNMENT CRITIQUE:

Use the Critique Checklist on pages 24 and 25 to monitor your progress. Grab a notepad, along with a sharpened pencil to capture good notes; then, rewind your tape to the very beginning. Listen to each recording in turn, and answer the Critique Checklist questions to the best of your ability. Listening to your voice carefully, write your answers on notepaper, then date and insert it in the middle of this chapter for safe-keeping – you'll need to refer to it later.

CRITIQUE CHECKLIST

1. **Volume.** Is my voice too loud or too soft?

2 **Pitch.** Does my voice seem artificially high or low? Does the pitch vary or does it stay pretty much the same?

3 **Rate.** Am I talking too fast or too slowly? Do I speed up toward the end of the message or maintain an even rate? Are there too many pauses, or none at all?

4. **Stress.** Do I over-emphasize certain words, or not emphasize enough, sounding bland? Do I stress the correct words that best communicate what I want to say, or do I stress certain words inappropriately? Does my voice rise at the end of sentences so it sounds as if I'm asking a question even when I'm not?

5. **Articulation.** Can the words be understood easily, or are some of them mumbled or swallowed? Does it sound as if I am working too hard to e–n–u–n–c–i–a–t–e e–a–c–h s–y–l–l–a–b–l–e?

6. **Resonance.** Does my voice sound thin and pinched? Does it sound as if I'm speaking to a large group of people?

7. **Quality.** Is my voice:

	Not at all	A little	A lot
Nasal or whiny	☐	☐	☐
Denasal or stuffed-up	☐	☐	☐
Breathy	☐	☐	☐
Tense or shrill	☐	☐	☐
Thin or squeaky	☐	☐	☐
Flat (no expression)	☐	☐	☐
Muffled (not much articulation)	☐	☐	☐
Hoarse or raspy	☐	☐	☐
Swallowed (coming from the back of the throat)	☐	☐	☐

8. Do I have a noticeable accent, speech challenge (like a lisp), or dialect of any kind? Is it slight? Does it affect the words chosen or obscure the meaning of what I'm trying to say?

9. Do I use proper grammar and pronunciation?

10. How would you describe the person who left this message? Is the person happy, sad, insecure, forceful, confident, scared, bored, persuasive? Was it an effective and accurate representation of how you wished to be perceived? Do you feel you spoke with authority, confidence and credibility in this context? Do you feel your messages would get return phone calls?

11. What did you like about these recordings? ("Nothing" is not an acceptable answer. Find something to like, even if it's "I like the fact that I got all my words out.")

12. What three things about these particular messages – the choice of words, certain vocal qualities, or the emotions expressed, etc. – would you like to change? How would you like to have sounded instead?

How many 'omigosh' experiences did you have? You have experienced the first of many opportunities you will have throughout the course of reading his book to evaluate your communication competence, particularly your ability to speak authoritatively, confidently and credibly. You will want to revisit this checklist after you have finished reading this book to reassess your progress. It will serve as your pre-post evaluation to show how close you have come to possessing the voice that means business.

> *The right to be heard does not automatically include the right to be taken seriously. To be taken seriously depends entirely upon what is being said.*
> *(Hubert H. Humphrey, Former V.P. of the United States)*

FREQUENTLY-ASKED
VOICE COMMUNICATION QUESTIONS

1. How can I be taken more seriously when I speak?
2. My staff tends to "zone out" when I'm talking. How can I keep their interest in meetings?
3. I hate my accent. How hard is it to eliminate?
4. My voice gets tired and hoarse when I'm on the phone all day. What can I do to prevent this from happening?
5. My manager says I'm too loud. Why don't I hear myself that way?
6. My supervisor always asks me to "speak up". When I do, I feel like I'm shouting. How can I project my voice?
7. Whenever I'm stressed, I can hear it in my voice. How can I sound more confident?
8. People say I have a great voice. How can I make it even better?
9. When should I use voice inflection…and how?
10. My voice quivers when I have to give a presentation. How can I sound more confident?
11. What's the ideal body posture for speaking?
12. I hear about "breathing from the diaphragm" when speaking. How do I know I'm breathing correctly?
13. I'm on the road over 200 days a year. How can I protect my voice when I travel?
14. What is the best thing to do when you lose your voice?
15. Why do we lose our voices? Can it be prevented?
16. Do our voices age?
17. How can I access my natural voice consistently?
18. I have nervous habits like throat-clearing and coughing before I speak. How can I stop doing this?
19. How can I eliminate the "ums" and "ers" when giving a presentation?
20. I hate hearing my voice on a recording! Why?
21. My manager often tells me I sound like I'm "whining". What does he mean?
22. When I'm angry, my voice is out of control. How can I regain control quickly?
23. I sound way too young, especially on the phone. How can I change my "little girl" voice?
24. I'm hoarse all the time. Sometimes my voice even hurts. What's going on?
25. My mouth becomes so dry when presenting. How can I avoid "cotton-mouth?"

> *The ability to speak is a short-cut to distinction. It puts (you) in the limelight and raises (you) head and shoulders above the crowd.*
> *(Lowell Thomas, radio broadcaster and journalist)*

VOICE OVERS

A Summary of Points to Remember

1. Your resumé may be your "calling card, but your voice is your "business" card.
2. Your voice is not a neutral characteristic, skill or trait.
3. The quality of your voice affects the quality of your career.
4. You must have the voice that means business, makes business and keeps business to remain competitive in today's highly-specialized marketplace.
5. Your voice is one of the critical business communications tools which determines how people respond to you and treat you.
6. Your voice can become a career-stopper, or a career-starter.
7. Use 'omigosh' experiences to improve your vocal, verbal and visual messages.
8. Speaking with authority is the ability to consistently use your voice, your words and your body language to communicate clearly, confidently and competitively.

Chapter Two

Your Voice Comes From Somewhere

*Your sense of "I" is your sense of who you are, whether you're tinker,
tailor, soldier, sailor, rich man, poor man, beggarman, thief, whether
you're a clown, strong and silent, a clinging vine…there's a certain
way of (speaking) with which you identify yourself and
which constitutes your image. (Alan Watts)*

If your eyes are the windows to your soul, then your
verbal and vocal awareness open those windows and
let the sounds of your soul out. What you speak, the way you
speak and how you say it tells the world about you. Your
identity is tied to your voice. Your very nature is revealed
through the spoken word, whether you are aware of it or
not. Every time you speak you reveal something about yourself.

By working with your voice, you will discover your natural voice – your true voice. You will learn that your voice is
as much a mirror as it is a window to your personality. It
reveals your fears, tensions and anxieties as well as your
aspirations, inspirations and moods. Your voice reveals who

31

you think you are, what you value, how you want the world to see you.

Exploring your voice will challenge you, confuse you, excite you. As you gain mastery of the power of your voice, you will notice its affect on others as they hear the real you. The more you pay attention to your voice, the more you will find that people pay attention to what you say. Your journey into more verbal and vocal awareness will pay dividends that go well beyond the mere exercises contained in this book. This increased awareness will extend to other parts of you – the social you, the creative you, the professional you, the *you* that knows you have uncovered an essential part of your own nature.

You will learn that you can connect with yourself through sound – the sound of your own voice. One of the simplest and most accessible ways to find your natural voice – your true sound – is to yawn. That's right! Try a gentle, slow yawn. Allow the yawn to be audible. Listen to yourself yawn. Yawn a few more times. Don't force the yawn. Just inhale slowly and exhale with a gentle yawn. Pay particular attention to where the sound ends. That final bit of "hot air" is where you will begin to find your natural voice.

Did you notice what your body did when you yawned? How it stretched? The downward push of your shoulders? The position of your eyes? The tilt of your head? Your relaxed posture? With this simple little exercise, you've begun to discover the voice that means business – your business, the self-expression business.

Where does your voice come from when you speak? The truth is it comes *through* the mouth, but not *from* the mouth. All human sound begins with an irresistible impulse from the brain – from a desire to communicate something out loud. This desire comes from a set of values and beliefs, and the will to express them. So your voice comes from who you are. It resonates from your very nature, your evolving self-concept.

When clients contract me for voice coaching, I start with their personal background because it often gives me a clue about where their communication problems originated. Two examples of this come very clearly to mind.

Recently, I was asked to speak to a plant manager who was having a tough time convincing workers to attend safety seminars. When I asked the department supervisors why, they said, "He sounds so angry and tense when he talks to us – always barking out orders and treating us as if we were dirt. Nobody wants to go to anything he recommends."

The plant manager's tense voice quality was coupled with body language that communicated insecurity and aversion (he habitually leaned away from people, stared at them with a furrowed brow, and never wore a smile.) His sour demeanor negated not only his authority but his important messages about plant safety. Attendance at safety seminars dropped and on-the-job accidents increased – in large part due to the plant manager's ineffective communication style.

When I asked him to tell me about his professional background, he shared that he had been a drill sergeant for twenty years. He was used to communicating vehemently to people under his command, especially about anything he considered a matter of life and death.

Working with him to relax his face, lower his volume or change his posture wasn't going to solve the problem. The issue was his military background and its influence on the way he treated subordinates. I suggested he speak to the department heads as if they were his peers and that he enroll them rather than order them. "This plant is your military base and your job is to conduct an organized operation with all your departments," I said. "Your team has to develop a plan of action that everyone will support. Agreed?"

Viewing the plant's department heads as equals rather than subordinates made all the difference. When he spoke to them again, he was firm and clear, but not overbearing. His communication was far more relaxed, with little excess tension or volume when he spoke. As a result, more departments signed up for safety seminars and the plant's safety record improved markedly.

The second example of understanding a client's background comes from the experiences of a woman I am working with as I write this book. As part of my classes, I have the students perform vocal exercises that mimic different emotional states. I ask them to speak as if they're excited, happy, angry, depressed, nervous and so on. It's a great demonstration of the ways our emotions affect how we sound. One of the female computer executives could not "sound-out" happiness. During the break, when I asked her about it, she began to cry. Then she said, "I just don't know how!"

This woman had the saddest voice I have ever heard. But when I questioned her about her personal background, I understood why her voice had so much pain in it. She came from a home with an abusive father and a depressed, alcoholic mother. She bore the brunt of her parents' difficulties for many years.

I've found that if people can imitate the sounds, words and muscular positions of certain emotions, they often find it easier to access their own emotions as well. "Kathy" literally had to learn to sound happy. She forced herself to use an upward inflection and a brighter, lighter tone. She practiced smiling at herself in the mirror, so her face muscles could get used to putting themselves into what was for her an unfamiliar position. And we worked with her choice of words. When someone asked "Kathy" how she was doing, rather than responding, "Okay" or "Fine" (with a downward inflection), she would say, "Just Great!" or "Outstanding!" or some other phrase that caused her to smile.

The difference in "Kathy" has been profound. Her voice, words and movements seem much lighter. Even her face has lost the downward lines that made her seem so much older than her thirty-five years. More importantly, "Kathy" told me her *inner* experience has changed. "I know all of these horrible things happened to me, but I've decided it's up to me how I live the rest of my life. I'd rather live it as a happy person than someone who's miserable all the time." In "Kathy's" case, changing her outside – the way she spoke and moved – had changed her inside as well.

> *Self-expression must pass into communication for its fulfillment. (Pearl S. Buck, Pulitzer Prize author and Nobel Laureate in literature)*

IS THE VOCAL YOU THE REAL YOU?

Your self-concept is a "generally" stable image that defines who you are and how you present yourself to the world. While your self-image can vary somewhat with the people and situations you encounter, it is usually remarkably consistent throughout your life. Your self-concept evolves from the interactions you have with others (what people tell you about yourself) and your own evaluation of your personal qualities, strengths and potential. Your self-concept influences what you think, how you view the world, how you act and what you say.

What you choose to accept as your reality determines what that reality is for you. It influences your behavior and your speech. While the chemical, neurological and anatomical systems you inherited from your parents create your genetic image, your reaction to your environment creates an on-going social image that determines people's perception of you. When people respond to your behavior, you, in turn, form perceptions based on these responses which reinforce, modify or change your concept of yourself.

Whenever you communicate, you are always communicating with your picture of the other person. How you manage that interaction through your verbal, vocal and visual "selves" determines your competence or incompetence as a communicator. Self-awareness is the key. It is this self-awareness, or self-preservation, that determines how you approach any given interaction.

Self-awareness, self-concept and speech interact synergistically so that the final result is greater than the sum of the parts. Your voice comes from self-awareness, which comes from self-concept, which comes from all that you have been before, done before and said before.

You will always be greater than the sum of your emotional, psychological and physical parts because your personality is evolving. Each day, you redefine yourself. We all do. And that redefinition changes the way we feel, act and talk each and every day of our lives. In order to speak with authority, confidence and credibility in any situation – to tell others, sell others, motivate others, teach others, collaborate with others, persuade others, delegate to others, and ask others – to do any and all of these things well, requires that the vocal *you* and the real *you* are the same *you*. It means you must have a realistic self-image – because that's where your true voice comes from whenever you express yourself.

I have included a brief treatment on self-image and self-concept in a book on voice communication because the act of interpersonal communication never occurs in a vacuum. Everyone has a self-concept. Each person's definition of that self-concept affects the quality of the voice that person uses to express his or her view of the world. Your voice, then, is the sound of your soul coming out into the world. It is your personality expressing itself in speech.

> *Crisis from dialogue occurs when (people)...fail to really address each other but turn away defensively, each within himself/herself, for the purpose of self-justification. (Renel Howe, theologian and author)*

WHERE DOES YOUR VOICE GO WHEN YOU SPEAK?

What does your real voice look like? There is an easy experiment you can perform to see what your voice looks like. It's based on the Bernoulli Effect which states that a gas (or liquid) in motion will exert less than normal pressure on its adjacent environment. It can easily be shown using your breath. Hold a piece of paper close to and a little below your bottom lip. Blow vigorously across the top of the paper. Notice how the paper rises slightly. That's due to the Bernaulli Effect. The air pressure above the paper is reduced by the blast of air from your lips causing the pressure below the paper to lift, or arc the paper.

This is the same aerodynamic principle that allows airplanes to take off, birds to fly and frisbees to lift and soar. Seeing the aerodynamic effects of your concentrated breath is a powerful image; but, the power of your voice, as well as your words, can move mountains, armies and nations. Accessing this power depends on breath control. We will speak more about breath and breathing later, but for now, I'd like to introduce you to a couple of breathing exercises that will help your voice speak with authority, sound confident and ring with credibility.

The purpose of the first exercise is to help you feel how your abdominal muscles move so you will breathe correctly when speaking. People who have voice problems often reverse the breathing process. They push the stomach *out*, instead of letting the stomach move *in* when they speak. The chief criteria for correct breathing when you are speaking is whether or not your belly is moving *in* and *out* slowly.

The average person breathes eight to twelve times each minute at rest, and more if under stress. The chest cavity is heavy and requires considerable effort to lift up and out. Chest breathing leads to hoarseness and a strained voice. Essentially, it means talking without enough air. And talking without air is a voice without power. Take a few minutes to do the following exercises:

Step I:
1. Lie down (face up) on the floor with a rolled towel or pillow under your knees to protect your back.
2. Place one hand on your belly (upper abdominal region).
3. Take a deep, slow breath in through your nose and feel your belly expand.
4. Now breathe out slowly through your mouth and feel your belly contract.
5. Repeat the process, focusing entirely on your breath and the rhythmic movement of your abdomen.

Step II:
1. Sit in a comfortable chair in a quiet room, one where you will not be interrupted. Place both feet on the floor.
2. Place one hand on your chest and the other on your belly
3. Take a deep breath in through your nose and feel your belly expand.
4. Count to five slowly and gently pull your belly in as you do so. Keep your chest as still as possible and focus on pulling your stomach in through the exhalation.
5. Hold your stomach in for another five counts.
6. Inhale once again through your nose.

7. As you slowly count to five again release the belly, keeping your chest still as before.

8. Repeat this process twice more, keeping one hand on your stomach and the other on your chest. Concentrate on how your belly muscle (abdominal muscle) tightens and relaxes.

9. Relax. Stretch a little. Take a deep breath and then exhale slowly.

> *Words are...the most powerful drug used by humankind.*
> *(Rudyard Kipling, Nobel Laureate in literature)*

YOUR TRUE VOICE IS JUST A BREATH AWAY

Vocal awareness begins with breath awareness. Correct breathing is fundamental for good speaking. Let's add to your awareness of proper breathing by completing this introductory exercise:

1. Stand or sit, whichever is more comfortable. Be aware of your posture. Your head should be erect and your face forward. Your shoulders should be relaxed and down. Hold your chest high, but comfortably and naturally. Your posture should be poised and erect.

2. Put one hand on your belly and the other hand in front of your mouth. Exhale a gust of air into your palm. Concentrate on your belly as it moves inward as you exhale.

3. Repeat this process twice more. Notice the warm gusts of air on your palm, and how your hand moves in and out on your belly. Make sure your chest does not move.

4. Take a deep breath. Slowly count to ten as you inhale, taking notice of the movement of your belly and the warm gust of air against your palm.

5. Relax. Roll your shoulders back and lower your arms to your sides.

This technique is invaluable for learning how to breath correctly. When you breathe correctly for speaking, you'll feel a calmness and confidence that wasn't there before. Practice this technique a few times each day beginning today. As you continue to practice proper breathing, your breath inhalation ability and controlled breathing in general will grow stronger.

If the slow breathing exercises make you feel a little spacey and dizzy, you are probably moving your chest too much. To correct this, pull your belly in less deeply and gently release your breath. You'll feel more control and will "teach" your chest to relax during your belly breathing. Slow belly breathing also reduces stress and is an excellent centering technique. If you want more information about the autonomic and parasympathetic nervous systems which affect breathing, there are many good books written on the subject. For the purposes of this book, I'm staying more practical than clinical to afford you the opportunity of moving quickly through this book so you can gain maximum benefit in a short period of time.

> *If your throat tires quickly when you talk...if you constantly clear it...if you are chronically hoarse, though you haven't a cold, don't smoke, and have nothing organically wrong with your throat — then you are not using your breath properly to support your voice.*
> *(Dorothy Sarnoff, singer and speech consultant)*

THE MEDIUM IS THE MESSAGE

Whether we speak with authority or squeak from inferiority, we use the same three communication tools: our voices, our words, and our bodies. Learning how to take charge of these tools can help you consciously shape the vocal, verbal and visual messages you're sending every moment. You'll be able to:

✔ develop the voice image and facility with language that will help you stand out in the crowded business world;

✔ identify your current vocal image and create your own natural *voice of authority*;

✔ learn easy-to-follow vocal exercises that will produce a flexible, dynamic, memorable voice;

✔ discover how to use language creatively and correctly, maximizing the impact of every communication;

✔ eliminate distracting speech habits, movements and gestures that negate the power of the message you wish to convey;

✔ create what I call your optimum "good-for-business" image;

✔ feel confident in any situation and achieve more personal and professional success as a result;

✔ Use the highest capabilities of your physical and vocal instrument to speak with authority, sound confident, stay poised and exude credibility.

Marshall McLuhan's famous assertion that "the medium is the message" may not apply to all forms of interpersonal communication, but it definitely applies to speech. Your voice can sell you successfully, or sell you short. The old maxim "you never get a second chance to make a first impression" is more true today than ever. First impressions are lasting impressions in today's nano-second business environment. Not being able to speak for yourself, or speak up for yourself, or speak with confidence and poise will cause you to lose many opportunities to sell yourself, not to mention your products and services. Your ability to project yourself starts knowing yourself. Having a realistic self-concept leads to a rich, practical and enduring self-awareness, and self-awareness affects the way you present yourself to the world – vocally, verbally and visually.

Frequent, thorough, open communication to every employee is essential to get the word out and keep walls from building within the company. And while face-to-face communication is more effective than impersonal messages, it's a good idea to vary the medium and the message so that no one (including top management) relies too much on "traditional" channels of communication. (William H. Peace, VP, KRW Energy Systems, Inc.)

VOICE OVERS

A Summary of Points to Remember

1. If your eyes are the windows to your soul, then your verbal and vocal awareness open the windows and let the sounds of your soul out.
2. The more you pay attention to your voice, the more you will find that people pay attention to you.
3. One of the simplest and most accessible ways to find your natural voice – your true sound – is to yawn.
4. What you choose to accept as your reality determines what that reality is for you.
5 Your voice comes from self-awareness, which comes from self-concept, which comes from all that you have been before, done before and said before.
6. Talking without air is a voice without power.
7. Vocal awareness begins with breath awareness.
8. Whether we speak with authority or squeak from inferiority, we use the same three communication tools: our voices, our words and our bodies.

PART TWO

THE VISUAL YOU

At the top of the magazine article was a picture of a well-stacked blonde at a construction site with a group of men around her while she read blueprints to them. I noticed her shoes were coordinated with her Gucci yellow hard hat. (Erma Bombeck, housewife and syndicated columnist)

Chapter Three

Putting Your Best Body Forward

By your finger-nails, your coat-sleeve, your shoes, your trouser-knees, by the callosities of your forefinger and thumb, by your expressions, your shirt or blouse cuffs – by each of these things your nature is plainly revealed. That all united should fail to enlighten the competent inquirer in any case is almost inconceivable. (Sherlock Holmes)

The most over-used phrases when it comes to discussing personal appearance are so much on target that I will repeat them here: "clothing makes the man (or woman)" and "you don't get a second chance to make a first impression." These sayings have always been true and they will always be true. People judge you on the way you look. They make decisions about what kind of person you are, your skills and competencies, your attitude, your intellect and your potential. While it is not uncommon to hear people say that inner beauty is the only thing that counts, research suggests that physical attractiveness and appearance play significant roles in determining your professional worth.

As countless surveys have shown, employers determine your potential based less on your resumé, academic credentials and work experience and more on the way you present yourself verbally, vocally and visually. Employers want to be sure you'll *fit in*, that you'll represent their organization in a professional manner, and that your business image mirrors their business image.

Is it fair that you should be judged on your appearance? Perhaps not, but the reality is you are – and usually in the first three minutes.

> *There is always the kid who has an aversion to clean clothes. He is allergic to creases in trousers, socks that have soft toes, underwear that is folded and sweaters you can sniff without passing out.*
> *(Erma Bombeck, housewife and syndicated columnist)*

THE 55% YOU SAY BEFORE YOU EVER OPEN YOUR MOUTH

Communication is defined by Webster as the "process by which meanings are exchanged between individuals." It is present in all good business and interpersonal relationships. You cannot *not* communicate. Whenever you are around people, you communicate in some manner – and usually in more ways than one. Although you communicate using words, you communicate equally by your tone of voice, your facial expressions, your body movements, the company you keep, how you are dressed and the environment you create around yourself.

Communication is not the same thing as information, just as speaking *to* someone is not the same thing as speaking *at* them. Communication is "exchanged meaning" (according to Webster) and information is "content." Communications researcher Albert Mehrabian conducted a series of landmark studies that determined how much body, voice and words contribute to this meaningful content. Although challenged by current researchers, his results still offer viable insights into how we communicate.

THE COMMUNICATION BUBBLE

Body =   55%
Voice =   30%
Words =   7%

The results of Mehrabian's study suggest that 55 percent of our total communications is body language; 38 percent is based on our voice; and 7 percent comes from the words we use. Other studies average out to a 60 percent body, 30 percent voice and 10 percent words ratio. The message is that a whopping 90 to 93 percent of our communications is not what we say, but how we look and act when we say it. It's in our gestures, our tone of voice, the way we dress and our attitudes. It's affected by our facial expressions, our posture, our height and weight, the distance between us and the person with whom we are speaking, and the way we make eye contact.

The message is clear: If you are to manage people's impressions of you, you must assume conscious control over the many ways your body communicates your emotions, character and values.
(Jo-Ellen Dimitrius, image consultant)

BODY BUSINESS

Wherever you go, whatever you do, you take your body with you. That is such a simple statement, but it's more profound that it appears. Your appearance on any given day can significantly affect the way people feel about you. Few people realize, or appreciate, how powerful body language is. "Those of us who keep our eyes open," says communications researcher, E. T. Hall, "can read volumes into what we see going on around us." This point is illustrated by a well-known story.

Once upon a time, according to researcher, Mark Knapp, Herr von Osten purchased a horse called Clever Hans. Hans and his owner lived in Berlin, Germany in the early 1900's. Herr von Osten taught Hans how to count by teaching the horse to tap his front hoof. Hans was a rapid learner and soon progressed from simple addition to multiplication, division and subtraction.

Soon von Osten began touring the countryside with his famous horse. Hans could count the numbers of people in the audience, the number wearing hats or glasses, the number of men versus women and children. He could tell time, use a calendar, recall musical pitch, and perform many other seemingly awesome feats. When von Osten taught his faithful horse an alphabet which could be coded into hoofbeat, Hans could answer virtually any question – oral or written. For a year and a half the clever horse baffled audiences all across Germany. It seemed that a common, ordinary horse had complete comprehension of the German language, the ability to produce the equivalent of words and numbers with his hoofbeat, and intelligence beyond that of many human beings.

Hans' successes were a result of pure and unadulterated observation. The stimulus Hans responded to was the tension in his trainer and the body language of onlookers when he tapped out the correct answers. Onlookers would relax and tilt their heads slightly when he got to the right answer, which became Hans' clue to stop tapping.

The story of Clever Hans is frequently used in discussions concerning the capacity of animals to learn verbal communication skills. Hans' cleverness was not in his ability to verbalize or vocalize commands, but in his good "horse sense" to respond to almost imperceptible and unconscious body movements on the part of his trainer and the audience. Hans was in the body business. He understood the relationship between a relaxed posture, head nods, his owner's tension and the correct answer. So if a horse can interpret body language by picking up certain non-verbal cues, human beings ought to be aware of the impact body language can have on their careers. Perhaps a *human* story can help make the point.

When Dan Rather replaced Walter Cronkite as anchorman for the CBS Evening News, his success seemed inevitable. He brought impeccable – and enviable – credentials to his new post (5 Emmys and a rating as the top White House correspondent in the history of broadcast news), and he had an extremely telegenic face, complemented by a commanding posture.

Unbelievably, the ratings began to drop, netting CBS third place behind ABC and NBC. Viewers were polled so CBS could assess the slippage. What they found was a comparison between the presentation styles of Walter Cronkite and his worthy replacement. The following list shows a comparison of adjectives which defined the TV images of both anchormen:

aloof	personable
anxious	calm
cold	warm
tense	relaxed
coarse	sensitive
pushy	good-natured
rigid	flexible
withdrawn	engaged
aggressive	conciliatory
detached	attentive
defensive	deliberate
ceremonial	informed
distracted	informal
mechanical	animated

The adjectives in the left column described Dan Rather and the ones on the right characterized Walter Cronkite. The problem was Rather's body language. As an aggressive reporter, he had to be firm and detached with a bias for action and urgency. But in his new role as CBS anchorman, he needed to project confidence, friendliness, and warmth. The remaking of Rather's nonverbal image literally saved his career. His changes, according to Gerhard Gschwandtner, included:

1. **Modifying his facial expressions:** He looked mechanical and ended each newscast with serious or stilted facial expressions. Coaching helped him become more animated. He added smiles which were almost nonexistent before.

2. **Improving his eye contact with the audience:** His preoccupation with the script caused him to look down too much, making him appear detached, cold and concerned with facts and not people. Getting used to the

teleprompter brought his eyes up to audience level, making him appear more personable and warm.

3. **Attending to his body position and posture:** His habitual, almost imperceptible, left to right body position shifts communicated nervousness or doubt and made him appear tense and defensive. He began to lean forward slightly to connect with the audience. Relaxing his neck and shoulders helped him appear more engaged and sociable.

4. **Evaluating his gestures:** Constantly keeping his arms close to his sides or pressed heavily against the top of his desk gave the impression that he was tense, unyielding, and a little too rigid. Increasing his hand and arm motions gave him a more relaxed, confident look. His news stories seemed much more personable and lively.

Altering his body language changed Rather's professional image from a hard-nosed, aggressive reporter to an amicably-engaged anchorman who was interested in keeping the public informed on news events that affected their lives. As a professional in your line of work, you must also project the right kind of image. Understanding the power of non-verbal communication can help you master body business, especially if you're in the business of selling your special talents, skills and expertise.

> *Many communications difficulties arise because we attack problems like James Thurber's dog, Jeannie, who tried to get out of a garage by digging through the concrete floor with one paw. We think people will be persuaded by our (common sense) or the force of our convictions — when in reality these glance off them like raindrops off a car roof. We have totally ignored the need to prepare the ground for the emotional climate which will make people listen to us, trust us and be persuaded by us. (Eli Djeddah, author)*

YOUR PHYSICAL APPEARANCE IS YOUR "VISUAL VOICE"

The way you dress and your over-all appearance is your "visual voice." People judge you by what you wear as well as what you say. Although the dress code for corporate America is more casual today, management still expects employees to dress appropriately. Your appearance is your "visual resumé" because it is the physical *voice* of your total communications package.

Every time you enter a room, meet a client or walk across the parking lot, you make a fashion statement. You strike an image by the way you walk, dress and appear to others. If your clothing attracts looks, make sure they're good looks, not disapproving ones. The wrong clothing at the *right price* is quite a price to pay if others voice what you wear negatively.

Your body language (gestures, facial expressions, posture, eyes) combined with your physical appearance are what I call "surface language" because people form immediate impressions of you. And the "surface language" of others makes an impression on you, too. One of the questions I ask during coaching sessions is: "Are you dressed for the job you want?" It is an important question. If you expect to get a promotion or land an important account, you must dress appropriately for the occasion. That means you shouldn't over-dress or under-dress. Research shows employers favor the conservative look which indicates practicality, dependability and a team attitude.

Dressing properly may not get you the job or the promotion, but dressing improperly can definitely keep you from being considered for advancement. Proper grooming, clothing and apparel add to your *visual resumé* Here are some general hints for both men and women in terms of dressing for success:

✔ Wear clean, polished, unscuffed, conservative and comfortable footwear.

✔ Invest in a really good haircut! Keep it conservative and current.

✔ Avoid chewing candy or gum in business settings.

✔ Keep clothing and jewelry accessories simple and classy.

✔ Pay close attention to personal hygiene. Tons of mousse/gel and truck-loads of cosmetics make you appear over-stated and under-managed. Keep teeth well-brushed and breath fresh.

✔ Limit use of perfumes and colognes. "Use a light touch."

✔ Make sure fingernails are well-manicured and hands well kept.

✔ Always assume a good posture – never slouch.

✔ Maintain a healthy weight. Learn how to wear clothing to accentuate the positive and camoflauge the negative.

✔ Keep clothing colors and styles reasonable and conservative.

✔ Avoid the disheveled look. Keep shirttails tucked in, scarves and ties tied, hair combed, beards and mustaches trimmed. Avoid frayed or worn belts, socks and hosiery, wrinkled clothing, soiled shirt or blouse collars. Always check yourself out in a full-length mirror before walking out the door.

Competition in the boardroom does not disappear with the removal of the jacket and tie.
(Mark Weber, Vice-chairman of Phillips Van Heusen)

UPDATE YOUR VISUAL RESUMÈ

One of the fun things I do with my coaching clients when it comes to improving their "visual voice" is to take them on what I call Cinderella or Prince Charming outings. We visit hair and nail salons, clothing and shoe stores, cosmetic make-up counters and jewelry stores. After our shopping, grooming, and complete make-over spree is over, I introduce each client to a mirror to see Cinderella or Prince Charming.

These outings have literally changed lives – and careers. With few exceptions, my clients thank me gracefully – and sometimes tearfully – for the positive changes in their appearance and attitude. What is truly amazing is that when their "visual voice" changes, their vocal voice changes, too – for the better. I have witnessed this transformation hundreds of times throughout my career. Your knee-bone is connected to your voice box, and so is your hairstyle, and your dangling earring, and your polished, scuffed-free shoes.

Do clothes really make the man or woman? I believe they are extensions of our personality, our subconscious desires and wishes. In addition to other "visual voices," our clothing connects with our inner voice, and our inner voice expresses itself in actions and words. When we look good, we feel good. And when we feel good, we sound good. So, don't turn your "visual voices" into visual vices.

Clothes make the man (or woman). Naked people have little or no influence on society.
(Mark Twain, publisher, humorist)

VOICE OVERS

A Summary of Points to Remember

1. You cannot not communicate.
2. Because you take your body with you wherever you go, you are always in the body business.
3. You physical appearance is your "visual voice." It is you visual resumè, your somatic cover letter.
4. The wrong clothing at the right price is a terrible price to pay if it compromises your "visual voice."
5. Update your visual resumè – dress for success.
6. Your knee-bone is connected to your voice box, and so is your hairstyle, your dangling earrings, your scuff-free shoes, and your wrinkled shirt or blouse.
7. Don't turn your "visual voices" into visual vices.

CHAPTER FOUR
EYE CUES

He speaketh not; and yet there lies a conversation in his eyes.
(Henry Wadsworth Longfellow)

Our fascination with the eyes has led to the exploration – and exploitation – of almost every conceivable feature of the eyes. Entire industries, from medical to cosmetic, devote billions of dollars to accent, shape and enhance the size, color and position of our eyes. And brows, lashes, rings and wrinkles are no exception. Eyes are a beautiful, expressive part of our faces, and are an important communication tool for gathering and sending information.

Throughout history, cultures all over the world have been preoccupied with the eye and its effects on human behavior and communication. How often have you heard or used one of these "eye-catching" phrases:

"It was an icy stare" – "Did you see the gleam in her eye?" – "He was afraid to look you in the eye" – "She's all eyes" – "We're seeing eye to eye now" – "The eyes are the windows to the soul" – "She gave you the evil eye" – "His eyes shout daggers across the room" – "If looks could kill…"

People pay close attention to the eyes. Societies establish eye-related norms. For example, you're not supposed to stare at strangers in public places; you shouldn't look at various body parts except under certain conditions; you shouldn't glance away frequently when someone is trying to speak to you.

We associate eye movements with a wide range of human expressions. A person who has wide eyes is usually considered to be frank, outgoing, naive, awestruck, terrified or surprised depending on the situation. People who look down a lot are considered to be modest, shy or unsure of themselves. Stares are associated with rudeness, coldness, combativeness and outright hostility. When people roll their eyes upward, they are usually communicating fatigue, disinterest, criticism or amusement.

> *Make certain the "windows to your soul" aren't clouded, giving the wrong information to the people in your life who are looking in. (Ken Cooper, speaker and consultant)*

PEOPLE CAN HEAR WHERE YOU ARE LOOKING

Our eyes reveal so much that I often tell my clients, "People can hear where you're looking. The narrowing of the eyes in response to a comment; a sudden raising of the eyebrows or a quick, flirtatious wink – all raise the decibel level of conversations." Anyone who's been on the receiving end of an icy stare knows what I'm talking about. Eyes can literally scream at you when they communicate disappointment, dissatisfaction, anger, fear or interest.

Let's have some fun. Adjourn to a place where you have access to a mirror – and privacy. We're going to give your eyes a little workout. I've arranged a list of eye behaviors with their corresponding emotions. Read the instructions for each emotion and then duplicate the emotion with your eyes. Let your eyes tell the story.

Emotions	Eye Cues
SURPRISE	Raise your brows so they are curved and high. The skin below the brow should be stretched. Your eyes should be wide open, with the upper lid open and the lower lid drawn downward.
ANGER	Lower your brows and draw them together so that vertical lines appear between your brows. Tense your lower lid and raise it slightly to accent the tension. Your eyes should be staring at the mirror without blinking.
FEAR	Your brows should be raised and drawn together. The upper eyelids should be raised, exposing the whites of your eyes. Your lower eyelids should be tensed and drawn.
HAPPINESS	You should notice crow's feet wrinkles fan out from the corners of each eye. Your upper eyelid should be relaxed and the lower lid should show wrinkles below it. The eyes should squint slightly.

NOTE: Each of these expressions can be ambiguous unless the entire face manifests the emotional signal representative of that particular emotion. Similarly, in everyday situations, whether you are at work, home or out-and-about, you will see what I call "facial blends" or "facial geography" where the eyes may say one thing and other parts of the face communicate something quite different.

As you've just demonstrated – quite dramatically, I hope – the eyes are truly the windows to the soul. You probably also noticed that your eyes didn't work in isolation. You probably found that other parts of your face supported your eye movements. When you looked angry you may have noticed that you leaned forward a little, tightened your lips, and tilted you head slightly. All body language is contextual. Whenever you try to interpret someone's eye movements, gestures, facial movements and posture, remember – all body movements, vocalizations and speech are contextual. Their correct interpretation depends on the particular situation and the people involved.

> *A hello-greeting should be a quick impersonal peck with all the passion of a sex-starved orangutan. Some kisses are so casual that while they are pecking you, their eyes are picking out the next kissee. (Erma Bombeck, housewife and syndicated columnist)*

WANDERING EYES CAN CAUSE PERMANENT DAMAGE

How many times have you talked to someone who broke eye contact with you to see who else was in the room or glance away in response to some other distraction? Have you ever attended a business meeting or luncheon where the person speaking rarely or never made eye contact with you? Not receiving the eye contact you think you deserve is frustrating. One of the chief offenses in interpersonal communication is the failure to provide and maintain appropriate eye contact.

Wandering eyes can cause permanent damage to any relationship. I have seen business deals disintegrate due to lack of eye contact. Applicants who fail to make eye contact during job interviews usually disqualify themselves immediately. Marriage partnerships and social friendships need eye contact to fuel the intimacy and camaraderie. Face-to-face communication means eye-to-eye communication. Without good eye-to-eye exchange, people engaged in conversation sense disinterest, feel neglected and lose trust in each other.

While I realize that no one looks at the person they're talking to 100 percent of the time, there seems to be a "proper" length of eye contact in any given situation. Obviously, the length and type of gaze will vary according to the background, purpose and personalities of the people engaged in the conversation. Because eye contact is so fundamental as a communication tool, I call eye *contact* an eye *contract*. When someone diverts his or her gaze inappropriately during face-to-face contact, he/she has just broken one of the most important "contracts" in the communication experience.

[General Eisenhower] and I didn't discuss politics or the campaign. Mostly we talked about painting and fishing. But what I remember most about the hour and a half I spent with him was the way he gave me all his attention. He was listening to me and talking to me, just as if he hadn't a care in the world, hadn't been through the trials of a political convention, wasn't on the brink of a presidential campaign. (Normal Rockwell, American artist)

EYE CARE MEANS YOU CARE

In communication terms eye care means paying attention to the amount of eye contact which occurs during human interactions. When you initiate eye contact, you are signalling that the communication channel is open. In some instances your eye gaze establishes an obligation to interact. For example, when you intentionally make eye contact with your waiter in a restaurant, you are obliging the waiter to respond immediately to your summons. On the other hand, you may recall instances in school or at work when your instructor asked a question for which you did not have an answer. Establishing eye contact in that situation was the last thing you wanted to do. You closed the communication channel. People behave the same way when they see someone they do not want to talk to coming toward them. Avoiding eye contact is a lot easier than obligating yourself to speak to or acknowledge that person.

Making eye contact means you want interaction. On the other hand, any time you want to disavow face-to-face communication, all you have to do is avoid eye contact. Of course, if someone forces eye contact, you may need to speak with authority, confidence and poise.

In addition to opening or closing communication channels, your "eye care" also regulates the flow of communication by providing turn-taking signals. The amount of eye contact can signal whose turn it is to speak next. For example, people seem to glance away at grammatical breaks, at the end of a particular thought, and when someone has just finished a sentence. Although glances at these junctures can signal that it is the other person's turn to speak, we also use these glances to see how we're being perceived and to see whether or not we should continue speaking.

Conversations are the process of speaking, then yielding, speaking again, then yielding again so each person involved in the dialogue has a chance to say something. Good "eye care" (the combination of appropriate eye contact and well-timed glances) helps facilitate the communication process. Good communicators manage this "eye contact choreography" in such a way that the speaking-yielding rhythm flows smoothly.

When people maintain eye contact with you when you're speaking, it usually means they're interested in what you have to say. However, if someone you're speaking to glances away occasionally, don't assume he/she is showing disinterest. Sometimes people have a tendency to look away when they are processing new or difficult information. This happens quite frequently during business meetings and performance appraisals when people feel pressured, unsure of themselves or threatened by the information.

We tend to make more eye contact with people we like, people we assign a higher status or role to than ourselves, and people we are attracted to romantically. The term "making eyes" is frequently used to describe flirtatious eye contact during dating and courtship activities. On the other hand, a gaze that turns into a stare is likely to induce irritation – if not outright discomfort or anger – if it is seen as inappropriate.

People who are extroverts usually maintain more eye contact than introverts. Sales and customer service people want to see how other people respond to their comments, instructions and advice. Accounting department personnel, engineers and researchers usually make less eye contact than their more outgoing counterparts. High status people also maintain less eye contact with subordinates and direct reports.

If you've ever been on the receiving end of a reprimand, you've no doubt experienced how people (supervisors, parents, military officers) use their authority to control eye behavior. For example: "Look straight ahead when I'm talking to you!" – "Look at me when I'm talking to you!" –

"Look what you've done!" That type of assertive, manipulative eye control is used to intimidate and dominate people. It is an effective disciplinary device, but that kind of forced compliance usually strains the relationship whenever it causes embarrassment, shame or guilt.

I have included this brief assessment on eye behavior because it is one of the most overlooked power communication tools. As a voice coach, I know that speaking with authority depends on seeing with authority. Engaging in an interesting conversation or speaking to an audience of one – or thousands – require the effective use of eye contact in order to build rapport, trust and relationships.

As a keynote speaker, I use eye contact to "connect" with my audiences because I want to establish that personal connection so that each member of the audience feels I am speaking to him or her personally. Although audience size prevents my making eye contact with each audience member, the members of the audience with whom I haven't made eye contact benefit because they know I could be speaking to them when I make a comment that strikes home.

I strongly encourage you to improve your "eye cues" when it comes to using and interpreting eye behavior. Both your personal and professional success depend on the quality of your "eye care."

> *Stand in front of a mirror and talk to the image you see. It helps you train yourself to make good eye-to-eye contact. (Larry King, CNN host and broadcaster)*

VOICE OVERS

A Summary of Points to Remember

1. People can "hear" where you're looking.
2. All body language is contextual. Your eyes are connected to the rest of your body.
3. Wandering eyes can cause permanent damage to any relationship.
4. Good eye contact is an eye contract. When someone diverts his/her gaze inappropriately during face-to-face contact, he/she has just broken one of the most important "contracts" in the communication experience.
5. Eye care means you care enough about what is being said to pay attention.
6. We tend to make more eye contact with people we like, people we assign a higher status or role to than ourselves, and people we are attracted to romantically.
7. People who are extroverts usually maintain more eye-contact than introverts.
8. The prudent use of good eye contact is one of the most overlooked power communication tools.

CHAPTER FIVE

LET YOUR FACE DO SOME OF THE TALKING

Your face is a book where men may read strange matters.
(Shakespeare, MacBeth, Act I)

Your face has awesome communication potential. Next to human speech itself, the face is the primary site for communicating information. It reflects your emotional swings, attitudes, values, preferences and personality. Because of its prominence and visibility, people pay considerable attention to facial expressions.

The human face comes in many shapes and sizes. People have round faces, square ones, rectangular and triangular ones; their foreheads may be high and wide or narrow and low, protruding or sunken; their complexions may be light, dark, coarse or smooth, wrinkled or blemished; eyebrows can be thick or thin, bushy or close; eyes may be balanced, close, far apart, recessed or bulging; noses can be long or short, flat or rounded, crooked or "humpbacked," "ski-sloped" or straight; lips are thick or thin; ears are large or small, close or jutting out; cheeks and chins can bulge or appear sunken.

The face is an amazing canvas of wrinkles, moods, and expressions. We make judgments about age, sex, cultural background, intellectual capacity, group affiliation and religious preference based on a person's facial characteristics. We see people with faces similar to people we know. We see well-sculpted faces, scarred faces, tanned faces and freckled faces, faces that look like models' faces, and faces that look like ten miles of bad road.

Faces provide a wealth of information about the "bearer". The human face is the mask you wear to reveal or conceal your true identity. It is the *you* you want to show the world. It is one area of your body, besides your hands, that remains exposed to the scrutiny of others. Friends, family, colleagues and customers recognize you by your facial characteristics. You are known by the face you wear.

> *The age lines and wrinkles on our faces are our experiential trademarks. (Cher Holton, management consultant)*

YOUR FACIAL GEOGRAPHY

Communications researchers estimate that we can make and recognize nearly 250,000 distinct facial expressions. Retail clerks have their die-cast smiles, talk show hosts unleash their hearty laughs, journalists report the news with expressionless faces, consultants and speakers wink at their audiences to build rapport, sales people give up their best smile no matter how bad the day has been, farmers and librarians pull their ears, school children wrinkle their noses, gamblers have their poker faces.

How often have you heard the following comments? "He or she has got to face the music" – "If you're enjoying yourself, why don't you tell your face?" – "Put on a happy face" – "It's as plain as the nose on your face" – "She cut off her nose to spite her face" – "He's got his game face on." All of these comments have evolved because people recognize how "telling" – if not outright incriminating – faces can be. Throughout my speaking and coaching career, I've probably seen all 250,000 facial expressions. You probably have, too! Let's see how your face can help or hinder your next sales pitch, performance review or conversation.

Although I'm dividing the face into parts to explain each particular facial characteristic, I'm going to qualify the following explanations with this caution: All body language, including facial expressions, occurs in a context. Interpreting someone's facial expressions accurately requires an assessment of that person's personality, the situation, and the person's body language. That being said, let's take a tour of the basic facial characteristics that affect the way people see you and the way you see other people.

A Quick Tour of Facial Geography

Forehead: A furrowed brow (along with other facial characteristics) can indicate puzzlement, tension, worry, concern, deep thought, or surprise. A sweating forehead can telegraph nervousness, fatigue or reaction to a warm climate. Perspiration due to effort is considered a positive sign while sweating brows due to stress and nervousness can be career stoppers.

Eyebrows: Heavily penciled, down-turned brows indicate concern and tension. Arched eyebrows give a more dramatic look and are viewed as indicating industriousness and interest. Over-hanging brows give people a brooding, even sinister look. Watch colleagues' eyebrows at work and see if you can "read" their brows.

71

Eyelids: People who have sleepy, hooded lids are considered to be cool, in control and detached. Winks can indicate warmth and charm, even playfulness. Winks without smiles usually say, "I've got a secret."

Excessive blinking: Repetitive blinking indicates shyness, nervousness and stress.

Watery eyes: Excessive watery eyes make us seem overly -emotional or weak. Contact lens wearers generally need to lubricate their eyes in dry business environments. If you are a contact lens wearer, you need to be careful when you wet your eyes so colleagues don't see you in a negative light.

Nose: Wrinkled noses indicate dislike, disinterest or disgust. Quivering nostrils usually mean anticipation, while flared nostrils indicate eagerness.

Mouth and lips: Smiles are the universal language of friendship and warmth. Although I'm tempted to rhapsodize about the smile – smiles can be deceiving as well as inviting. Tight-lipped smiles can indicate diplomacy, but not agreement. A smile drawn out to long can indicate irritation and even contempt. Basically, however, smiles communicate pleasantness and invite amicability.

As you can see from the above summary of facial cues, good communication, in most circumstances depends on the facial expressions you use to give and receive feedback. Your expressions convey that you have a personality, that you understand what's going on in the conversation, and that you are either present or detached from what is being said. Research has shown that the average person learns from 85 to 90 percent by sight, 5 to 7 percent by hearing, and 3 to 5 percent by touch. Sight has a tremendous impact on your ability to give and receive feedback. Facial expressions lead to impressions, and the impressions people form of you can be either positive or negative, depending on your facial geography at the time. Remember, your face is connected to your knee-bone and your knee-bone is connected to your voice-box and your voice-box is connected to your – I think you get the picture.

Some people intentionally disguise or control their facial expressions to hide their true feelings or play games with people's emotions. Faces can conceal as much as they can reveal. They are masks, facades, casts of countenance. But one thing is for certain – people remember faces before they remember names. So be yourself. Let your face represent who are really are. Your face may be a mask, but let it be a clear one. Make sure that what you're saying with you face matches what you're saying with the rest of your body.

> Wrinkles should merely indicate where smiles have been.
> (Mark Twain, writer and humorist)

FLEXING YOUR SMILE MUSCLES

Believe it or not, it's easier to smile than frown. According to some researchers, it takes 43 muscles to frown, but only 17 muscles to curve the lips into a smile. Other researchers claim it takes as few as five pairs of facial muscles to smile, and as many as 53 to frown. This number doesn't include the neck muscles or associated muscles that could be used by purposefully exaggerating an expression. Regardless of the precise number of muscles used, smiles cause fewer muscles to contract and expand than frowns.

You've no doubt seen smiles that can light up a room. Julia Roberts, Britney Spears, Brad Pitt, and Leonardo Di Caprio all have dynamic smiles. Think of people you know at work, at church, in school and in volunteer organizations who have awesome smiles. Their smiles signal warmth, happiness and joyfulness. And smiles beget smiles. It's hard not to smile when you see one.

Is it possible that a simple thing like curving your mouth into a smile can help you feel better, perform better and think more clearly? And can moping and frowning create negative attitudes which can lower your spirits, work performance, and thinking ability? Current research says yes. If you're interested in more smile research, consult the bibliography at the end of this book. I don't have the space to do it here except to say that the bottom line about smiles is that smiles are therapeutic – and they help produce laughs which are even more therapeutic.

When people laugh, they relax, they loosen up a bit. A good laugh requires people to use their lungs and heart to get the necessary blood and oxygen into the body. The very act of laughter forces oxygenated blood through the blood stream where it circulates through the muscles, organs and brain. Laughter rejuvenates the entire body inside and out. It elevates the immune system and strengthens the spirit.

Some recent research suggests that if you are feeling depressed and gloomy, you can change your physiological and psychological disposition simply by biting on a pencil, pen or your index finger. I'm not kidding! People in the study were asked to hold a pencil or pen lengthwise between their teeth to create a sort of forced smile. Some people used their index finger by laying it across their teeth lengthwise. When they bit down lightly on the objects, their mouths formed into a smile. (Try it. Use a pencil or your finger and see if you don't grin just enough to hold the objects.) The reason it works is because the same facial muscles you normally use to smile are triggered. The facial muscles that form your mouth into a smile somehow "fool" the body into secreting all those wonderful happiness chemicals. Isn't that awesome?

You'll probably find this next statement awesome, too. People can "hear" you smile or frown over the phone. I'm sure you've experienced it. Smiles lighten the voice and frowns lower it. You can see for yourself. Form your lips into a smile. Now say: "Hi, how may I help you?" Now downgrade your smile into a frown. Say: "Hi, how may I help you?" Did you hear the difference? When you "smiled," your greeting voice was pleasant, moderate to high pitched and amicable. When you "growled" your greeting – even when you used the same words – your voice sounded a little crabby. Your tone was lower and you probably sounded like you had just lost a chance at winning the lottery. So, flex your smile muscles, both on and off the phone.

Smiles truly are contagious. They are infectious communication devices. They will help you get customers and keep customers, attract friends and keep friends, build rapport with colleagues and deepen relationships with colleagues. Smiles bring out the best in people. They are essential ingredients in rekindling people's spirits. Smiles enrich those who give them and those who receive them. They foster goodwill in business and are the countersigns of enduring business relationships.

> *A smile cannot be bought, begged, borrowed or stolen…because it is something that is of no value to anyone until it is given away. (Rabbi Samson Raphael Hirsch)*

VOICE OVERS

A Summary of Points to Remember

1. Human beings have over 250,000 distinctive facial expressions, so let your face do some of the talking.
2. The face is an amazing canvas of wrinkles, moods and expressions.
3. You are known by the face you wear. It is your mask, façade and cast of countenance.
4. Your facial geography can change in an instant from happy, joyful, confident expressions to looks of sadness, fear and anger.
5. It takes 43 muscles to frown, but only 17 muscles to curve the lips into an infectious smile.
6. Laughter elevates the immune system and rejuvenates the entire body.
7. People can "hear" your smiles and frowns on the phone.

CHAPTER SIX

CHOOSE YOUR MOVES:
CREATING A POWERFUL GESTURE BANK

We all, in one way or another, send our little messages to the world…And rarely do we send our messages consciously. We act out our state of being with nonverbal body language. We lift one eyebrow for relief. We rub our noses for puzzlement. We clasp our arms to isolate ourselves or to protect ourselves. We shrug our shoulders for indifference, wink one eye for intimacy, tap our fingers for impatience, slap our foreheads for forgetfulness. The gestures are numerous, and while some are deliberate…[T]here are some, such as rubbing our noses for puzzlement or clasping our arms to protect ourselves, that are mostly unconscious. (Julius Fast, psychologist)

Arms and hands are second only to the face in expressing your wants, desires and needs. They can help define how your body looks during aerobic exercise, animate your speeches, or transmit detailed "speech" to the hearing impaired. They can summon a waitress with the check, hug a child, or juggle popcorn and drinks at the movies. They can provoke a fight, embrace a friend, and perform instant repairs on a bike. As a speaker and voice coach I employ a considerable repertoire of gestures to accent my voice and facial expressions. I choose gestures that create a dynamic learning atmosphere, hold the audience's attention and amplify the message I was contracted to deliver. During my coaching sessions, all of my gestures, posture and body movements are designed to help clients feel comfortable, relaxed and ready to learn.

Standard social gestures are called *emblems* by communications researchers. Hitchhikers stand at roadsides holding their thumbs up to catch a ride. The peace sign, palm out and index and second fingers extended, has long been used to communicate love, peace and brotherhood. Sports teams proudly hold index fingers up to proclaim "We're number one." The "high-five" gesture (two people face each other, raise one or both of their hands, palms facing each other and smack hands to show jubilation) is a celebratory *emblem* millions of people recognize. Striking the Heismann Trophy pose by standing, lifting one knee waist high, cradling an imaginary football, and stiff-arming the air is a gesture that says, "I'm the best at what I do."

We also use gestures that are instructional. I have a dear friend who always asks for the check at restaurants by first catching the eye of the waiter and then scribbling in the air as if he's signing an imaginary credit card receipt. He has never had this sign misunderstood domestically or abroad. Men often describe a remarkable female shape by tracing the appropriate curves in the air. Women similarly outline the desired muscular male physique by diagraming a V-shaped chest figure.

We are all natural mimics to some extent, so it's not surprising we imitate other people or use our hands to tell a story. You can watch people sitting around a conference table in a meeting room and tell who is leading the discussion. It'll be the one using hand gestures to amplify the message. The presenter may use one or both hands to trace the flow of information or list the main points of discussion. After the meeting someone may imitate the presenter's message by mimicking his/her hand movements, voice and other associated body language.

Gestures are an important part of your "total body works." Understanding them is just as important as understanding facial expressions, eye behavior, and vocal and verbal variety. Like spoken language, gestures and body movements have dialects and regionalisms. While voice has intonations (pitch, intensity, tempo, resonance, and the like), gestures have a sort of paralinguistics all their own: *emblems* (head nods, yawns, thumbs up or down signs, shaking a fist, clapping hands together), *regulators* (handshakes, a good night or good morning kiss, smiles, glances), and *adapters* (scratching, rubbing, picking, preening). I included this sketch so you can appreciate the complex language of gestures. It will serve as a good introduction for the rest of this chapter.

> *Just as your tone and volume of voice must be related to how close you are to someone, so must your gestures. Scratch your nose if it itches, make a gesture if it illustrates a point or a story, or clasp both hands behind your back. The point is to communicate clearly.*
> (Steve Allen, comedian and entertainer)

KEEP A LEVEL HEAD

We've discussed the head as a communication tool in Chapter 5 when we assessed facial expressions. However, I have reserved head posture for this chapter so I could discuss its "language value" as it applies to body image. The head is the uppermost part of your body, therefore, the most visible communication tool. This may sound contrite, but the best way to stay ahead of your competition is to use your head. Use it in a dignified way. Use it authoritatively. Here's how:

When you tilt your head slightly to the side during a conversation, it indicates your interest and attention. It can also mean you are deep in thought or are evaluating what is being said. One way to show your introspection is to tilt your head when you are asked a difficult question. You may know the answer immediately, but your answer will seem more thoughtful if you appear to be thinking about it. Besides, it will be taken as a compliment by the questioner because you devoted so much effort toward answering his/her question. On the other hand if you over-use this technique, you will appear unsure of yourself, or hesitant to answer.

Head nods are an excellent communications tool, but can mean different things to different people. For women, a head nod typically indicates agreement, while for men a head nod says, "I'm listening, but don't necessarily agree."

When you want to encourage someone or invite someone to continue talking, nod your head several times at important junctures in the conversation. I use head nods during my coaching sessions to say, "Yes, I'm listening" or "I hear what you're saying." Swayed, side-to-side head movements usually mean "no" or "I disagree." However, slow swaying movements, coupled with lowering your eyebrows, generally means "I'm not sure I understand you."

When people jerk their heads back suddenly and frown at the same time, they are implying disagreement or agitation. One of my coaching clients over-used this behavior and was seen as belligerent and uncooperative. Over the course of several weeks, we analyzed his head jerk response and found he used it when he didn't understand something or was caught off guard by someone's comment. Eventually, we were able to modify his reaction so that his non-verbal signals matched his emotional reactions.

People show surprise or shock by lurching their head forward and then putting it back quickly. It means "I've gotten your point" or "you've got to be kidding." On the other hand, when you draw back your head slowly and drop your chin, you are showing a growing interest or amazement at what someone just said or did.

Downward tilts of the head are associated with shyness, depression and low self-esteem. Habitually looking up slightly may give the impression you are snobbish, arrogant, or snippy, and that you walk around disdainfully, with your "nose in the air." Looking straight ahead with a level head and erect posture shows confidence and composure. It is part of the "look that means business."

> The just argument against a stupid head is a clenched fist. (Neitzsche, philosopher)

POSTURING YOUR SUCCESS

What do you think when you see someone with stooped or bowed shoulders? Are they tired? Depressed? Could they be self-conscious or afraid? Do they seem down-troddened or over-burdened? Are they sad? Do they appear hopeless? Although stooped shoulders and bowed heads can mean many things, they're usually considered negative. A stooped posture is not a confident posture. It tells prospective employers, business associates, and customers that the person they're doing business with or want to do business with appears negative, lackadaisical, lazy or lost.

People carry tension in their neck and shoulders. Raised shoulders usually indicate tension, apprehension and stress.

How many times have you caught yourself driving home from work and noticed that your shoulders were up around your ears? Have you noticed how colleagues tighten and raise their shoulders when they hear news of lay-offs, reorganizations or mergers? The tension of the day and the stress of rush hour traffic cause both our shoulders – and blood pressure – to rise. I'll bet your shoulders begin to creep up on your drive to work! When my clients feel under stress, I encourage them to relax the shoulders, take a deep breath, and say things like "It's okay. I can handle this" – "Lower your shoulders and take a deep breath" – "I am cool, calm and collected." All it takes is being aware of your body's reaction to stress and tension.

Keeping your chest slightly forward and your shoulders slightly back shows pride and confidence. Your posture will improve automatically and you'll notice definite improvement in your breathing as well. Depending on your other "body scan" signs, your confident posture can appear too forceful, tenacious or even belligerent. Generally, however, this is the posture that will "posture" you for success.

The way you look when you're seated is important, too. In general, the more relaxed you are with shoulders slightly back and a straight, but not arched back, the better you will appear. Slouching when you're seated is not a good career move. It affects your voice control and quality as well as your professional image. The way you rise from your seated position affects your professional image, too. Leaning forward as you stand and unfolding on the way up makes you look sleepy and unenthusiastic. Use your leg muscles to lift yourself quickly and keep your back straight. That's the look of confidence, enthusiasm and poise.

Maintaining an erect but relaxed posture when you stand creates the image of someone who is in control, confident, self-disciplined and businesslike. Standing correctly and confidently sends the message that you are comfortable with responsibility, accountability and the demands of work in general.

Stand with both feet firmly planted and shoulder width apart. Distribute your weight equally over both feet. Placing your weight on one foot throws your shoulders out of alignment and gives you the Leaning Tower of Pisa look. Leaning towers are tourists attractions, but leaning executives and managers attract negative perceptions like, "How can he manage this project if he can't stand on his own two feet?" – "She's got that look that says she's just doing her job, don't ask her to do anything else."

Leaning on your feet also leads to shifting your weight to the other foot and back and forth, giving the impression that you're tired, disinterested or over-due for a restroom break. Stand confidently so you exude the look of professional competence.

> *Nothing is more revealing than movement.*
> *(Martha Graham, dancer, choreographer, educator)*

HAND SIGNALS

One of the questions most asked by my clients is "what do I do with my hands when I speak?" It's an important question because hand movements must complement your facial expressions and other body language so you can get the right message across. Hands are full of communicative potential. We hold hands with those we love. We say grace by joining hands. Pointing your index finger at someone says, "I want you" or "I'm acknowledging you." Shaking your finger at someone means "Stop that" – "I don't like that" or "Hey, that wasn't necessary." Poking your finger on someone's chest can cause a fight. Extending your index finger, pinky and thumb means "I love you in American sign language." When you hold the same gesture parallel to the floor, then float it upward, it's the sign for an airplane.

We can use the edge of our hands to make forceful karate chops or strike the edge of a table with a clinched fist to make a point. Shaking our fist is usually a sign of anger. It can also demonstrate a playful acknowledgement of someone's cleverness. Holding you palms out, extending your arms and raising your shoulders generally signals "I don't know"; or "whatever." Raising your hand and waving it signifies a greeting or good-bye.

A tightly-closed fist is the universal sign of force. It is not seen as being positive in business environments. Fists generally mean anger, disagreement, strong irritation, combativeness, frustration, hatred, fear and forcefulness. Using your fist to pound your palm, pound a desk for emphasis, or pound a colleague sends the same message: aggression. That type of behavior is considered totally unprofessional and will destroy your business image.

Limit the jewelry you wear. A couple of rings and a wrist watch are quite sufficient. Through the years several of my coaching clients have worn jewelry on every finger and thumb. There's a lot to be said for individuality and love for adornment, but excessive jewelry usually has negative connotations in a business environment. Fingernails should be well-kept and manicured. Dirty fingernails in office environments give the impression you are the kind of person who takes a bath every Saturday night whether you need it or not. Biting your fingernails signals nervousness and lack of self-confidence. Nail length should at least extend to the end of the fingertip for both men and women. Women who wear nail polish should choose conservative colors, and ensure that the polish covers the entire nail.

> *We respond to gestures with an extreme alertness and, one might almost say, in accordance with an elaborate and secret code that is written nowhere, known by none, and understood by all.*
> *(E. Sapir, communications researcher)*

WHAT'S IN A HANDSHAKE?

I don't know about you, but I enjoy firm handshakes. There's nothing worse than shaking a limp hand. In the business world, handshakes can make or break a business relationship. It is usually the first physical contact people make with associates, clients and prospects. Firm enthusiastic handshakes are momentum-building. They communicate warmth, confidence and interest. Wimpy shakes create whimpy relationships. They indicate aloofness, indifference and lack of credibility. Handshakes, where one person places the other hand on top of the joined hands is a bit too intimate (in a professional setting) and send the wrong message.

Generally speaking, handshakes should be firm, corresponding grips should match "squeeze-ability," and appropriate eye-contact should be maintained. The "politician's handshake" offering the hand in an "L" shape so only the fingers can be grasped, is the classic example of a poor handshake. On the other hand (excuse the pun), if a "crusher" gets your hand in his vice grip, you may have to cry for mercy.

One of the executives I coach initially had a wimpy, what I call "limp biscuit" handshake. Although he was a strong, tall, beefy guy, his handshake was more like a jelly shake. When I mentioned it to him, he explained that he used to injure people's hands when he shook hands with them. He added that he didn't know his own strength so he adopted a more wimpy handshake. At the risk of putting my "microphone-holding" hand in harm's way, I worked with him over a period of a few sessions specifically devoted to handshakes.

I am pleased to say that both of our "shaking" hands are fine and that his handshake is firm and strong, but not crushing. I am also pleased to report that each of my coaching clients has the "perfect" business handshake. In addition to my clients' improved voice quality, handshakes are one of the trademarks of our client-coach relationship. I focus on improving the image of each of my clients from head-to-toe.

> *Your handshake is your bond. As far as I'm concerned, a handshake is worth more than a signed contract.*
> *(Victor Kiam, former owner, Remington Products, Inc.)*

KEEP A LEG UP ON YOUR COMPETITION

Although we spend a large amount of our business hours sitting, we also have to use our legs as well as our brains. Generally speaking, men cross their ankles in front of them or assume the "figure 4" position (one ankle-on-opposite-knee) when they are in a sitting position. Women tend to cross their ankles under the chair or cross their thighs while sitting slightly catty-cornered on the chair. The best advice I can give both men and women in regard to "leg care" is that people rarely make important decisions when one foot is off the floor. So keep a leg up on your competition by keeping both feet firmly on the floor.

> *I always wear slacks because of the brambles and maybe the snakes. And see this basket? I keep everything in it. So I look ghastly, do I? I don't care – so long as I'm comfortable.*
> *(Katharine Hepburn, actress)*

> *People use their power to communicate at about one-fifth capacity; we often just stand there, face expressionless, arms hanging slack, eyes stationary, voice droning out language noises, getting neither at nor into each other the message to be communicated. We are disembodied voices; our bodies are only somnolent casings of skin, hair, flesh and bone.*
> *(Carl Croneberg, author)*

VOICE OVERS

A Summary of Points to Remember

1. Arms and hands are second only to your face in expressing your wants, desires and needs.
2. We are all natural mimics to some extent, so it's not surprising we imitate other people.
3. Like spoken language, gestures and body movements have dialects and regionalisms.
4. While voice has intonations, gestures have a sort of paralinguistics all their own.
5. Keeping your head level and maintaining a good posture signify you are "on the level" and contribute significantly to the look that means business.
6. Depending on your other "body scan" signs, your posture can help give you that extra something, a presence which says "I am someone that is used to winning."
7. Slouching, whether you're seated or standing, is not a good career move.
8. Wimpy handshakes create wimpy relationships.
9. Creating a powerful gesture bank means improving your image from head-to-toe.
10. People rarely make important decisions when one foot is off the floor.

PART THREE

THE VOCAL YOU

In an attempt to achieve a vocal "ideal," people can develop nodes, polyps and ulcers of the larynx – and be well on their way to committing vocal suicide in an effort to achieve vocal desirability.
(Mark L. Knapp, communications professor and researcher)

CHAPTER SEVEN

IS YOUR VOICE MEMORABLE, FORGETTABLE OR AWFUL?

A singer is nothing other than a vocal athlete.
(Dr. Clark Rosen, otolaryngologist)

In his bestselling book, *How to Develop Self-Confidence and Influence People By Public Speaking*, Dale Carnegie says that "we are evaluated and then classified by four things in this world: by what we do, by how we look, by what we say, and by how we say it." I have already covered "how you look" in chapters three through six. you can improve "how you say it" by working on the vocal you. This chapter begins that important process so you can develop the "voice that means business."

If you are like most people when it comes to projecting a professional image, you probably spend a lot of time and money buying the right clothing, attending the right schools, writing the perfect resumè, staying politically correct, associating with the right people, and so on. Yet, when was the last time you spent some quality time improving your voice? Again, if you're like most people, you can't remember. The only way you will ever develop the "voice that means business" is – to get serious about developing the voice that means business. The fact that you've read this far means you want to improve your vocal quality.

Can you imagine a news anchor, singer, Hollywood actor, public speaker or voice coach (how's that for putting myself on the line?) whose livelihood depends on voice quality having a weak or squeaky voice, poor diction or the inability to breathe properly. People who speak or sing for a living polish, protect and pamper their voices. They know that people make judgments about their competence, credibility and star power based on the strength and quality of their voice.

National headlines tell us about the voice problems that have plagued many of the world's high profile people. Julie Andrews underwent laser surgery to repair her vocal cords. Country singer, Kathy Mattea needed surgery to repair a small blood vessel in her throat. Kenny Rogers, Larry Gatlin, Crystal Gayle, Reba McEntire, Michael Jackson and Whitney Houston have all consulted throat specialists.

People who need their voices take care of their voices. Who needs their voice? Everyone. Doctors, lawyers, CEO's, human resource professionals, telecommunications executives, salespeople, consultants and trainers, the clergy, customer service reps, homemakers, parents, bank tellers, day care administrators – all need a voice that works. And *you* need a voice that works, too!

Is your voice memorable, forgettable or awful? Is it too nasal, high-pitched and deep-throated? Is your breathing shallow or even reversed? Do you have your share of sore throats? Is your voice hoarse and strained? Do you feel an inordinate amount of throat tension? Hoarse, raspy voices are memorable, but do you want to be remembered for that? Strong up-lifting voices like Dr. Martin Luther King's, and "money" voices like Natalie Cole's and, of course, James Earl

Jones' textbook voice are memorable. Does your voice sound awful? Is it hoarse like Bill Clinton's voice, or deep-throated and flat like Henry Kissinger's? Is it nasal and thin like Cyndi Lauper's or breathy and weak like Woody Allen's?

Voice problems can turn people off. People are repelled by irritating, loud, weak, coarse and boring voices. People react emotionally to sound. If the radio signal in your car is clear, you'll listen. If it is filled with static, you'll change the station. If the reception on you wireless phone is clear, you'll continue to use it. But if it is contaminated with static or fades in-and-out, you'll end the conversation and change service providers. The same thing goes with your voice. If you vocalize clearly, they'll listen. If you have poor vocal quality, you will lose people's interest.

> *Many women have been made painfully aware of the negative effects their high-pitched voices have on their career. That's unfortunate because the competitive attitude of most career women is at a fever pitch.*
> *(Lillian Glass, Ph.D., voice communications consultant)*

VOCAL SUICIDE

If your voice is "talking" to you through its hoarseness, nasality and soreness, it's telling you it's in trouble. Minor voice problems can become major voice problems. Throat lozenges, gargles and sprays are only temporary fixes. They take care of some of the symptoms, but not the causes of vocal difficulties. In my experience, over-the-counter medications only mask the symptoms and make it easy for people to postpone voice care.

Many clients who come to me have misused and abused their voices in a number of ways. Communications researcher, Mark Knapp, calls it "vocal suicide." I can't think of a better way to describe that kind of abuse. Vocal suicide is the intentional or unintentional misuse or abuse of your voice. It results from long term damage to the vocal cords. Continued misuse and abuse causes nodes, polyps or contact ulcers on the vocal cords.

Voice *misuse* involves using the wrong pitch, tone, volume, speaking rate and breathing support to speak comfortably and normally. Voice *abuse* means that you may injure or already have injured your voice by making a habit of excessive shouting, screaming and loud talking. Like most of our physical ailments, voice damage sneaks up on us. It may come from cheering for our favorite team, talking on airplanes, speaking in a large room without a microphone, trying to be heard over loud machinery, the TV, other people or traffic noise.

Most of us have had laryngitis at one time or another. Our voice seems strained, hoarse or choked. We are plagued with short, choppy breathy spells. Some people develop what is called spasmodic dysphonia or a strangled voice which lingers. Do you want to hear what spasmodic dysphonia sounds like? Try this quick experiment. Exhale completely so that you have forced all of the air out. Now, without breathing in, start counting aloud. You will not need to count very long to feel the choked sound of your voice.

The only way you'll ever change from a troubled voice to your natural voice is to take conscious care of your voice. Chances are your habitual voice is not your "real" voice. Very few clients have brought their real voice to the first coaching session. Usually, it takes six to eight weeks up to three to four months to "capture" someone's real voice. The amount of time, of course, depends on the individual's interest, enthusiasm, vocal health and support system.

One of the first voice exercises I ask my coaching clients to perform is the "um-hmmm" test. I review proper breathing techniques and then ask them to use the midsection breath support (allowing the stomach to move in)and say "um-hmmm," which is the sound you make when you agree with someone. I instruct clients to keep their lips closed and repeat "um-hmmm" without forcing the sound out. After a number of "um-hmmm's" I have them add the number "one." So they'll say, "um-hmmm one...um hmmm one" a few times.

Once clients are comfortable with that sequence, I'll ask them to say "um-hmmm two...um-hmmm three" and so on until they count to five. The "um-hmmms" eventually begin to bring out their natural voices by the end of the session. People usually "find" their natural voices fairly quickly. *Keeping* it is quite another matter. Over the next couple of sessions, I help clients move from their habitual voice to their natural voice. It takes practice, patience and perseverance. After all, people have carried their "vocal vices" with them for years, and old habits are difficult – but not impossible – to break.

Major changes in your voice are similar to major changes in your looks, clothing and buying habits – they get noticed. For example, I coached a telecommunications manager with Sprint who spoke with a thin voice. She sounded similar to the TV character Georgette on the Mary Tyler Moore show. Physiologically, thin voices occur when the level of the glottis is high and the pharyngeal cavity is closed which causes the insecure-sounding thin voice.

When I helped her find her natural voice, her husband had difficulty adjusting to the new woman we had created. She projected a whole new image. She sounded more confident and self-assured, more grown-up. Her professional image improved – and so did her income. At home she used her newly-acquired natural voice to sound business-like and dipped into her girlish thin "vocal disguise" when she wanted to "disarm" her unsuspecting husband. Her double vocal image, it seems, has made life very interesting at home.

Finding the *natural* you is discovering – or should I say recovering – the *real* you. Voice therapy, like any other therapy, is an inner journey. It connects with subconscious parts of you which need expression. A good self-concept is selling yourself on yourself. Good vocal awareness and vocal quality help you sell yourself to others.

You'll never sell any product that is as important as selling your authentic self. Selling your professional worth, your leadership qualities, your uniqueness, your competence and capabilities, your potential – are your most basic selling jobs.

> *Stop committing voice suicide. The prevalence of troubled or failing voices is of epidemic, but unrecognized, proportions. (Dr. Morton Cooper, celebrity voice doctor)*

WHAT ARE YOUR VOCAL VICES?

Your voice has the same capacity to *touch* others with its variety, resonance and power as a musical instrument. It can create excitement, joy, reverence, comfort, attachment, introspection, wonder and loyalty – if you *play* it well. One of the first steps you can take is to assess your current voice. You will find that you have a unique voice. It is an instrument that has an infinite variety of pitch, tones, volumes and ranges. Let's examine a few of your bad habits that contribute to an unhealthy voice. Place a *"Y"* for yes and an *"N"* for no to the left of each of the questions below:

VOCAL VICES

1. Do you eat chocolates, drink carbonated sodas and/or water, or drink caffeinated coffee?
2. Do you drink ice water immediately before you speak?
3. Do you breathe from your chest area when you talk?
4. Do you have a habit of rushing your words, clearing your throat, sniffling, sighing, yawning, coughing or clicking your tongue too often?
5. Are you uncomfortable with silence during conversations?
6. Has anyone ever told you that you speak too loudly, slowly or softly?
7. Does your voice sound hoarse, strained, nasal, throaty, tired?
8. Do you seem to have your share of allergies, postnasal drip, hay fever, tonsil infections, and sinusitis?
9. Are you in the habit of screaming, yelling or raising your voice when you're angry or upset?
10. If you've ever had laryngitis or a nasty cold, did you try to talk or whisper even though your throat hurt?
11. Do you smoke?
12. Do you seem to have indigestion a lot?
13. Are you used to working under a high degree of stress and tension?
14. Have you ever had the feeling of a foreign substance or "lump" in your throat?
15. Even when you aren't suffering from a cold or the flu, do you notice chronic tickling, soreness or burning in your throat?
16. Do you have too many "phantom" toothaches?
17. Do you notice a lot of mucus in your throat which forces you to swallow frequently?
18. Do you repeatedly lose your voice if you "talk too much?"
19. Does your voice seem clear in the morning then tired or raspy toward the end of the day?
20. Are you now or have you ever been a stutterer?

If you answered *yes* to three or more of these vices, you are not taking care of your voice. If you answered *yes* to ten or more you are a prime candidate for vocal suicide. The amount of vocal damage you are inflicting upon yourself is considerable. Unless you begin to eliminate some – preferably all – of these vices, you will never improve the quality of your voice. Your voice will work if you work. The vices mentioned above are lifestyle vices. Changing your lifestyle can change you voice style.

> I won't take somebody into voice therapy unless they stop smoking. You're in essence pouring poison over your vocal cords with every inhalation.
> (Dr. Celia Hooper, vocal pathologist)

> Just as some women are beautiful without adornment, so this subtle manner of speech, though lacking in artificial graces, delights us. (Marcus Tullius Cicero)

VOICE OVERS

A Summary of Points to Remember

1. The only way you'll develop the "voice that means business" is to get serious about developing the voice that means business.
2. People who speak and sing for a living polish, protect and pamper their voices.
3. If you vocalize clearly, people will listen. If you have poor vocal quality, you'll lose people's interest.
4. If your voice is "talking" to you through its hoarseness, nasality and soreness, it's telling you it's in trouble.
5. Lozenges, gargles and sprays only mask throat problems.
6. Vocal suicide is the intentional or unintentional misuse or abuse of your voice.
7. Voice misuse involves using the wrong pitch, tone, volume, speaking rate and breathing support to speak comfortably and normally.
8. Voice abuse occurs when people injure their voice by making a habit of excessive shouting, screaming and loud talking.
9. Like most of our physical ailments, voice damage sneaks up on us.
10. Your voice has the same capacity to "touch" others with its variety, resonance and power as a musical instrument.
11. Lifestyle habits that contribute to an unhealthy voice are called vocal vices.
12. Your voice will work if you work.

CHAPTER EIGHT
VOCAL STATIC

In much of your talking, thinking is half murdered. (Kahlil Gibran)

Good vocal health, just like good physical, mental and emotional health, is a key predictor of your total health and well-being. Your voice is the audible sound of your inner health. Believe it or not, the quality of your voice indicates the quality of your inner life. It mirrors your inner being. Uncovering your natural voice opens the door to expressing who you really are. It gives you vocal permission to "sound off," to exercise your vocal right to be heard, understood and accepted for who you are.

Vocal awareness starts with a recognition of what I call *voice static.* We create "static" every time we rob our voices of their natural tone, quality and resonance. We clothe our voices in nasality, hoarseness, soreness, tension, dryness and breathiness. All of these negative vocalizations are voice impairments and they dilute the effectiveness of one of the most powerful communicative tools on earth – the human voice.

He replies in nothing but monosyllables. I believe he would make three bites of a single cherry.
(Francois Rabelais)

THESE TEN VOICE ROBBERS STEAL YOUR VOICE

Your speaking voice has many special abilities: listen-ability, sound-ability, understand-ability, project-ability, believe-ability, sale-ability, emotion-ability, intellectual-ability, calm-ability, excite-ability, credibility, and, above all, you-ability. All of these qualities are positive qualities. Unfortunately, too many people rob their voices by turning the positive aspects of these qualities into vocal static.

One quality I haven't mentioned is the very quality that can help save your voice – resilience. It is the voice's flexibility and resilience that make it so malleable, useable and marketable. That's the good news. The bad news is those same qualities lead to the voice's misuse and abuse, robbing it of its vibrancy and naturalness. We're going to examine each of these robbers briefly so you can see how they can *steal* your professional image.

I have given each of these "criminals" names and divided them into pairs. Pairing them has to do with the anatomy and physiology of the human voice. They are opposites both anatomically and physiologically and affect the voice differently and, unfortunately, negatively.

BREATHY OR TENSE VOICES:
THE SEXPOT VS. THE DRILL SERGEANT

Both breathiness and tenseness result from the amount of air which passes through the vocal folds and the muscle tension of the folds. Breathiness is caused by too much air getting through the folds. A tense voice is caused by excessive muscle tension of the folds. Anger, excitement, exhaustion and nervousness can cause breathiness. Breathiness can also be intentional when the attempt is to convey sexiness. Marilyn Monroe is the ultimate Hollywood version of "breathiness with a purpose." Michael Jackson probably has the most recognizable breathy male voice.

A healthcare manager I worked with had a breathy voice. She knew she was not taken seriously at work. Although she was quite competent and energetic, her "Marilyn" voice, as her co-workers called it, interfered with her credibility. When we found her natural voice, it was a much more forceful, resonate voice like Jacqueline Kennedy Onassis' breathy, patrician voice.

A tense voice retails the image of sternness, impatience and authoritativeness. It unnerves the listener and creates an atmosphere of defensiveness and agitation. The TV character, Barney Fife, is a classic example of comedic tenseness. Loretta Swit's character, Major Houlihan, on the TV series Mash is another example. A tense voice robs you of the ability to garner quick support or build rapport, whether you're talking to friends, family or colleagues at work.

FLAT OR THIN VOICES:
THE BORE VS. THE LITTLE KID

Voices which sound flat use the low pitch range and open the pharynx up so much that inflection is impossible. People who do this sound monotonous, boring and disinterested. You can compliment people on how nice they look, but if you don't sound enthusiastic or believable, you're better off not saying anything at all. The classic example of flat, monotone voices are Howard Cosell, Henry Kissinger and Sylvester Stallone. People who sound flat frustrate us. When they speak they have a sort of glazed sleepy look, and the fascination of a slow-dripping faucet. We doubt their credibility and find that they fry our nerves very quickly. A flat voice can be very effective, however, when someone is angry and screaming at you. A monotone voice in these instances can indicate that you are in control and poised.

Thin, shrill, screeching voices like the Betty Boop and Mr. Magoo characters usually label the people who use them as immature, insecure and nervous. They are associated with weakness, stupidity, vulnerability and lack of depth.

NASALITY OR DENASALITY:
THE WHINER VS. THE ALLERGY SUFFERER

The only redeeming quality I can think of associated with a whiny voice is exemplified by Fran Drescher's nasal New York City whine. The character she played used nasality effectively to portray the manipulative Nanny. In the entertainment business the voice she used is called a "money voice." Someone else who has made a career out of nasality is Andy Rooney who ends each week's 60 Minutes spot whining about something. Whiners talk through their noses instead of their mouths. A tight-jawed, ventriloquistic speaking manner is not the kind of voice that "wins friends and influences people." Usually the object of unkind jokes and ridicule, whiners are constantly plagued by rejection and inhospitableness.

A Nortel executive learned he was being ridiculed behind his back because of the way he talked. He had such a nasal voice that people didn't know whether he was serious or kidding about certain business matters. He asked me to help rid him of his nasality. Fortunately he didn't have a cleft in the palate (roof of the mouth) or a short palate. His problem was he never opened his mouth when he spoke. He would have made a great ventriloquist. We were able to "denasalize" him and correct several additional vocal vices that were affecting his career. We still keep in touch and his voice quality is awesome.

Denasality sounds like your voice is clogged up. It is the allergy sufferer's voice or the cold sufferer' stuffy voice. Lily Tomlin's TV character, Edith Ann, is a show biz example of a de-nasalizer. Denasalizers sound ill and congested. It's the kind of voice that no one wants to stand too close to. People who sound this way may have enlarged adenoids, blocked sinuses or a serious physiological problem. A checkup by an ear, nose and throat specialist would determine if medication or surgery is advised.

FRONTAL OR THROATY:
THE SNOB VS. THE JOCK

Frontal voices are characterized by pursing your lips so that you sound pretentious or phony. The arrogant, lofty vocal quality of Mr. and Mrs. Howell on Gilligan's Island demonstrates snobbishness in its most comedic form. The blue-blood, preppy quality of pretentious speech sounds like success, status and sophistication, but "smells" like pure, unadulterated puffery. A vocal image which exemplifies arrogance is not the kind of voice that attracts business and keeps customers happy.

Harsh-sounding, coarse, husky voices that sound strangled, swallowed and croaky are examples of throaty vocalizations. They sound gravelly, as if the person has food or tobacco in his/her mouth. Harsh, raspy voices are often the result of allergies, bronchitis or years of smoking. Throaty voices also come from vocal abuse and misuse. Jimmy Stewart and Mae West gravelled and had very distinctive "money voices." Without star quality status, most people who rasp and gravel sound painfully uneducated, uncultured and unemployable.

MUFFLED OR OROTUND:
THE TEENAGER VS. THE PREACHER

Muffled voices are simply sloppy voices. Elvis Presley was a good example. Muffling or mumbling is caused by poor articulation, lowering your voice too much, covering your mouth with your hand when you speak, or looking away during conversation. Mumbling forces people to work too hard to understand you. It's an irritating habit. People associate muffled voices with a lack of confidence, laziness, insecurity, incompetence, dishonesty, intellectual numbness, self-consciousness and a host of other demeaning perceptions. Muffled voices are anti-business voices. Inability to articulate the features and benefits of your products and services is the inability to stay in business.

I worked with a brilliant engineer at Nortel who mumbled his way through three reorganizations until he found himself severely compromised by his voice. His new manager thought his mumbling subordinate was trying to sabotage an important project by refusing to share valuable information. At the time he came to me his job was on the line. I was able to identify his chief vocal problem immediately – his teeth looked awful. He mumbled because he was embarrassed about his teeth. On my advice, he confessed and apologized to his manager for his speaking impediment, assuring the manager that he was not trying to sabotage the project or his career. Then it took a dentist, an orthodontist and me over a year to transform a muffled voice into a model voice.

Orotund voices are those outrageous voices that intentionally elongate s-y-l-l-a-b-l-e-s and v-o-w-e-l-s to a ridiculous extent. Ernest Ainsly, Robert Shuller and many of the tele-evangelists use the orotund style to sound Biblically authoritative.

> *I try to avoid pompous language. Some people use it as an oral status symbol to impress others. Others use it because they've simply forgotten how to talk in simple, clear, everyday terms. (Larry King, CNN broadcaster)*

VOCAL AEROBICS FOR VOCAL STATIC

I have included the following Vocal Static Exercises to help you begin to clear your vocal "channels." By now you probably have a good idea how much vocal static you generate. Start with the tip for your particular voice robber, then add as many of the other tips to your *posse* as your time and interests allow. I have provided additional "static busters" in Chapter 11, Vocal Aerobics. Are you ready to get some of the static off your *air* time?

BREATHINESS BUSTER

This is a simple contrast exercise. Place your hand in front of your mouth and give a big sigh or yawn. Now pronounce each of the following *h* words, beginning with the monosyllables of *h*, plus a vowel followed by one-syllable *h* words:

ha	hack	had
hail	hair	half
hall	halt	hand
hard	has	hat
hate	have	he
head	hear	help
hem	hen	herd
hip	him	hit
high	her	how
hug	heal	hurl

Feel the air on your hand. Now remove the "h" and say the words. The breathiness is eliminated.

TENSE SENSE

Tense throat muscles create an artificially high, thin voice. Learning to relax the throat, jaw and neck muscles can help to reduce vocal tension.

1. Sit in a comfortable chair or on the floor. Head, neck and back should be in alignment. Close your eyes and breathe easily. Count to five slowly, taking a deep breath in through your nose, out through your mouth.
2. Yawn and sigh two or three times. Feel the jaw and throat relax.
3. Slowly take your right ear toward your right shoulder until you reach a mild point of tension. Then slowly lift it back to center. Repeat on the left side.
4. With an "easy" or "confidential" voice (as if you are revealing a secret) count from one to five. Glide through the numbers.

FLAT CHAIR PULLS

This exercise is designed to develop your stomach muscles so you can project your voice. It is a well-known exercise in the voice coaching industry. Sit in a chair and place both arms beside you so you can pull up on the seat. Alternate pulls and releases seven times in succession. As you pull and release, say "Ah" for as long as you can. You'll feel the vocal tones resonate in your stomach each time you execute your pull and release movements. Repeat this process seven times. You can vary this process by pushing instead of pulling on the chair.

VOCAL INFLATION

If your voice is flat (no inflection or pitch variety), these exercises will be invaluable.

I. Choose your favorite word with two or more syllables. Say it using the following emotions: sadness; joy; boredom; anger; fear; surprise. Listen to the pitch changes!

II. Read aloud and tape record a children's book, such as one by Dr. Suess. It's hard to read one without using vocal variety. Have your children or grandchildren (or neighborhood children) listen. They will be your best critics.

THIN WICK

This simple technique, practiced three or four times each day will strengthen your vocal support muscles quite nicely. Sit or stand, maintaining good posture. Take a few normal breaths in through your nose, releasing through your mouth. Now pretend your index finger is a candle. Hold it about twelve inches from your face and direct a gentle stream of air toward it as if to extinguish the imaginary flame. Form your lips into a whistling position as you do this.

If you aren't sure you're getting your breath to the "candle," wet your finger and try blowing on it again. You should feel the cool evaporation affect on the moistened finger. Repeat this process three or four times. Now hold the "candle" eighteen inches or so from your face and repeat the above process. Finally extend your arm as far as possible, with the top of your hand facing you and send a gentle stream of air toward the "wick." The further away your finger is from your face, the more you must use your groin and stomach muscles.

NASAL NUT

People are nasal because they don't open their jaws wide enough to resonate sound properly. They clamp their jaws and limit the functions of the palate and oral cavity. This exercise will help set jaws in a more normal position:

Pretend you have a peanut (or your favorite nut) between your back teeth, propping your jaws slightly open. Remember, we're only pretending you have a nut in your mouth. Keep your jaws propped open and place your middle or index finger and thumb on the bridge of your nose. Say "ba, ba, ba, ba, ba, ba, ba." Repeat that sequence once. Now clench your jaws so your back teeth touch firmly, not forcefully. Pinch your nose again and say "ba, ba, ba, ba, ba, ba."

You should have felt a difference. If you felt a noticeable buzz the first time you did this exercise, open your jaws wider. Pretend you're holding an unshelled walnut and try saying "ba" again. If you still feel a buzz, you may want to consult a specialist to see if medical intervention is warranted.

DEEP THROAT MASSAGE

This exercise takes care of both frontal and throaty static. One of the best cures for these vocal robbers is to recite polysyllabic words slowly, making sure each *syl-la-ble* is pronounced clearly Try these for a start:

articulation	monotonous
communication	rationalization
enunciation	telecommunications
conversation	colloquialism
characterizations	conversationalist
hyperbole	insubordination
exaggeration	polysyllabical
pretentiousness	straightforwardness
talkativeness	ungrammatical
vocalizations	uncommunicativeness

Here is another simple frontal voice buster. All you need is a mirror and your thumb and forefinger. Gently press your lips back with your thumb and forefinger as you talk. Watch and listen as your voice changes from snobbish to stylish.

DENASAL NO MO

This exercise should help you feel 'resonated." Say this sequence of ma's and mo's as rapidly as you can for about fifteen seconds. Start with *ma.* Say it for fifteen seconds, Then say *mo* for fifteen seconds. Then say "ma, mo, ma, mo, ma, as fast as you can for ten seconds. Lightly place your fingers on either side of your nose, and feel the buzz.

MUCH ADO UNDONE

One of the simplest techniques to shorten orotund speaking habits is to repeat slowly, clearly and methodically the vowel sounds "a, e ,i, o, u" over and over again. Start with a dozen repetitions, then try two dozen.

Another way to shorten the syllables is to repeat a tongue-twisting phrase rapidly which forces you to articulate each word concisely. Say the following phrase as fast as you can without mumbling, running the words together or lingering on a word:

A pair of partially paralyzed pickled parasites perched passively playing peekaboo panicked a pauper peeling peppered pastries purposefully partly plugged.

All of these exercises are designed to clear your vocal static. Voice static means that your vocal difficulties need to be corrected naturally or medically. If any of the symptoms I have outlined in this chapter persist, I strongly recommend your seeking professional help. Voice disorder prevention starts with vocal awareness, and vocal awareness can save your voice and your career.

A great many people think that polysyllables are a sign of intelligence. (Barbara Walters, TV commentator and journalist)

VOICE OVERS

A Summary of Points to Remember

1. Good vocal health is just as important as good physical, mental and emotional health.
2. Good vocal health is one of the key "predictors" of your total health and well-being.
3. Vocal awareness starts with a recognition of voice static. We create "static" every time we rob our voices of their natural tone, quality and resonance.
4. Negative vocalizations are voice impairments and they dilute the effectiveness of one of the most powerful communication tools on earth – the human voice.
5. It is the voice's flexibility and resilience that make it so malleable, useable and marketable.
6. Voices filled with vocal static are simply anti-business voices.
7. Vocal static means your vocal difficulties need to be corrected naturally or medically.

CHAPTER NINE
VOCAL HICCUPS

Mind your speech a little, lest you mar your fortunes.
(William Shakespeare)

A treatment of vocal awareness would not be complete if I didn't include a section on what I call "vocal hiccups." The kind of "hiccups" I'm referring to are outrageous vocal behaviors like talking too fast, too slowly or too loudly; yawning or belching; frequent swallowing, sighing or coughing; blowing hair out of one's eyes; heavily-marked breathing and grunting; over-extended pauses; sneezing, sniffling or blowing your nose; licking, biting or smacking your lips; nasal snorts; habitual throat clearing; whistling through your teeth; clicking your tongue or teeth; lisping or stuttering; and so on. Such vocal tics or "bloopers"are generally associated with nervousness, dissatisfaction or a lack of confidence and self-control.

Talking too quickly or slowly: People who talk too fast give the impression they are excited, pushy or nervous. They remind you of the speedy sales pitches aired on TV or radio commercials. Speed talkers generally talk so fast they run words together or sound choppy. One woman I coached was a call center director for a telecommunications company. She was a bright, extremely attractive woman who was highly respected for her managerial skills, but criticized for her speed talking which approached 225 words per minute. Listening to her was quite an experience. Normal speaking rates are between 120 and 160 words per minute. After several months we were able to reduce her rapid fire speaking to 140 to 180 words per minute. Although her speaking rate was still a little fast, she was much more intelligible, varied her pace, and sounded enthusiastic instead of pushy.

People who speak slowly seem to take forever to finish a sentence. They don't usually pause excessively, they just talk as if they have all the time in the world to get their point across. They appear dull-witted, less confident and less sure of themselves than their rapid-speaking counterparts. On a more positive note, however, slow speakers are perceived as being more friendly and approachable.

Loud talkers: Most people are disturbed by loud talking of any kind. Loud talking creates a sound barrier. It damages vocal cords and relationships. Some people talk loudly because they have a hearing loss. Most people talk loudly because they're used to raising their voice over various kinds of noise.

A television anchorman with a major network approached me after an experience he had at Wrightsville Beach in North Carolina. He was sitting on a blanket talking to several friends when he noticed that people nearby were looking at him. He thought they recognized him since his face was a familiar face on TV. They would look in his direction, then glance away, look, then glance away again. Finally, one of the beachcombers headed in his direction. Thinking the fan wanted his autograph, he retrieved one of his note cards from his beach bag and waited for his fan's arrival.

The visitor was not a fan, nor did she recognize him. But she did have a lot to say. She was extremely angry with him. She told him he had total disregard for people around him who were trying to find some peace and quiet. She had come to the beach to get away from people like him. "You talk too loud," she told him. "You sound like a circus barker!" To add insult to injury, he told me, everyone sitting nearby applauded the woman. He also added that several people had collected their belongings and left, reinforcing the woman's point.

He admitted that he knew he talked too loudly and that several of his colleagues had mentioned it to him from time to time. But he had never been embarrassed like that before. It was that embarrassment that brought him to me. After a few months, we got his volume under control and cleaned up a few more of his vocal vices for good measure.

Another example will help you see how disastrous a high-pitched, fast-talking voice can be to your career: Early in my career I was approached by a young reporter who was working at an NBC affiliate in Cleveland, Ohio. She hosted a teen dance program, and did some reporting as well. She approached me and said, "Linda, I'm a good reporter, I know my stuff, but nobody takes me seriously. The station sends me out on fashion stories, teeny-bop pieces, instead of anything hard-hitting. What can you do for me?"

She came across as a very intelligent person and looked great on camera. However, she was not taken seriously because her voice was thin, high-pitched and had a consistent upward inflection. As a result, she sounded like a teenager. She also had a few minor articulation and speech clarity problems – including difficulty pronouncing certain letters and words.

She was committed to doing whatever was needed to improve her image. She constantly practiced the exercises I gave her and there was a noticeable change in her vocal quality and articulation in a few weeks. A few months later, she left Cleveland for Boston for a more high-profile reporting job. Since then, she has been both a reporter and anchor for such well-known TV programs as *Attitudes* (on the Lifetime Channel), *Hard Copy*, and *American Journal.* One of her greatest journalistic coups was interviewing mass murderer, Jeffrey Dahmer – certainly a far cry from her teen dance program days.

Yawning and belching: These obnoxious vocal behaviors interfere with your message and are extremely irritating to the people you're talking to, whether you're speaking to one person or a conference ballroom full of people. Some people use these crude sounds for comic relief. Others use them to be obnoxious or inhospitable. Eliminate these etiquette busters from your vocalizations.

Frequent swallowing, sighing or coughing: Infectious sinusitis, postnasal drip and allergies can affect how you speak. Medical conditions like gastroesophageal reflux (the regurgitation or backflow of corrosive stomach acid forced up into the esophagus) affect speech. When the toxic overflow reaches the chest, it causes a fiery sensation known as heartburn. Tiny amounts bubble to the throat and irritate the vocal cords.

Swallowing and coughing caused by throat and sinus infections are tolerable to listeners sympathetic to your health condition. However, these habits still detract from the quality of your voice and the impact of your message. These problems can also be symptoms of more serious health issues, so please seek medical attention if you are experiencing any of them.

Nervousness can cause coughing and excessive swallowing, giving people the impression you are unprepared, anxious or incompetent. Excessive sighing communicates disinterest, boredom or disrespect.

Blowing hair out of one's eyes: Allowing personal grooming habits to interfere with vocal quality is distracting for both you and your listener. Blowing hair out of your eyes can be a simple grooming matter or indicate huffiness, disgust or anger. If it's a grooming matter, it detracts from the message. If it's an emotional signal, it accents the message. Either way, this outrageous blooper needs to be cosmetically removed from your business vocabulary.

Heavy breathing and grunting: These hot-air bloopers generally indicate disgust, dissatisfaction, fatigue or poor health, and are usually viewed negatively. They could also be symptomatic of a health challenge.

Over-extended pauses: Lengthy pauses or too many pauses interfere with a natural speaking rate, and keep listeners waiting and wondering why you're so indecisive … or…absentminded…or…if you're suffering from…attention deficit disorder.

Sneezing, sniffing or blowing your nose: Colds and allergies help create these annoying vocal bloopers. Clearing congestion from nasal passages interrupts your message and generally requires the use of tissues or handkerchiefs which call attention to your "nasal emergency."

One of my favorite stories about vocal bloopers is the one comedian, Steve Allen, tells on himself:

> *Be yourself. Speak naturally. People will be fully sympathetic – once they decide they like you – if you stammer or happen to tip over a glass or forget what you were going to say.*

> *I once delivered a talk while suffering from a bad cold. At one point, I simply had to say: "Ladies and gentlemen, if you'll forgive me, I'm suffering from quite a heavy cold and – believe it or not – I'm just going to have to stop here for a moment and blow my nose. If you'll excuse me…"*

> *I turned away, blew my nose vigorously and then got back to work. There was no reaction from the audience at all except a slightly sympathetic chuckle.*

I share this story to illustrate this point: Steve Allen took the risk because he was comfortable in front of audiences – and comfortable with himself. If anything, the circumstances probably heightened the audience's trust and sympathy for the comedian, helping them see him as being human and not just a famous entertainer.

Sympathetic ears, however, will lead to harsh tongues if you sneeze, yawn or belch too often during conversations.

Licking, biting and smacking your lips: All three of these bloopers give others the impression you've either eaten a meal that's stuck with you, enjoy the taste of your lip gloss or chapstick, or are nervously waiting for your next meal. Biting your lips ruins your appearance and draws attention to the blemishes on your lips as well as the "blemishes" in your conversation.

Habitual throat-clearing: Throat-clearing can be caused by any number of things which have one thing in common – choppy speech. Colleagues and customers alike will interpret this blooper as demonstrating nervousness, uncertainty or insecurity. Colds and throat infections can also cause you to clear your throat. Try substituting a light cough, accompanied by a hard swallow, instead of throat clearing. It is less abusive and will break the habitual behavior. If you have a persistent dry throat, I recommend your consulting an otolaryngologist.

There are plenty of medicines available for treating colds, flu, cough, catarrh (inflammation of a mucous membrane causing increased mucous flow) and bronchial and laryngeal problems. I use them as quick fixes for my throat problems. If I experience a severe throat infection, accompanied with voice loss, I see my laryngologist immediately. Clearing my throat too often in my business would lead to clearing business from my calendar. If that happened too often, I'd be out of business.

Whistling through your teeth: This practice is generally considered out of season unless you're rehearsing for a singing part in the classic holiday song, *All I Want for Christmas is My Two Front Teeth.* It means you're forcing too much air out between your teeth. It gives the impression you're missing a few teeth or have a cracked or chipped tooth that needs dental attention. Whistle while you work, on occasion, but never while you speak.

Clicking your tongue or teeth: Clicking your tongue gives the impression you've got something caught in your teeth or gums or are enjoying the last hint of a taste of something you ate. Clicking your teeth might work for sending a Morse Code message, but you'd probably be better off saying what you want to say. One thing is for certain, you can't click and talk at the same time.

Lisping or stuttering: Stuttering is a communications challenge that may have its roots in emotional and physiological traumas associated with early childhood. The great American actor, James Earl Jones, has always been painfully shy – as well as a stutterer. He responded to an interview about his stuttering in a *Los Angeles Times* article (Dec. 19, 1995) and I have included it here to help you see that every one of these vocal bloopers can be corrected if you are motivated enough to *voice* your voice. He says:

> *My voice is a gift that often doesn't work. I still have difficulty getting thoughts out, so my goal is to say something with clarity. I left the church at the age of 14 because I couldn't do Sunday school recitation without the kids laughing...But the great Olympic runner, Wilma Rudolph, had serious leg problems. (Dancer) Gwen Verdon had rickets as a child. Demosthenes put pebbles in his mouth and became a great orator. If you acknowledge a weak muscle and exercise it, it can define your life.*

Very much aware of his vocal weakness, James Earl Jones chose to find his true voice. He could just as easily have decided to define himself as a stutterer and accept the impediment. Millions of people enjoy his awesome baritone richness today because he chose to develop the voice that means business.

He mouths a sentence as dogs mouth a bone.
(Charles Churchill)

VOICE OVERS

A Summary of Points to Remember

1. People who talk too fast give the impression they are excited, pushy or nervous.
2. Normal speaking rates are between 120 and 160 words per minute.
3. Loud talking creates a sound barrier. It damages vocal cords and relationships.
4. Medical conditions like gastroesophageal reflux affect speech and should receive medical treatment as soon as possible.
5. Throat-clearing can be caused by any number of things which have one thing in common – choppy speech.
6. If you experience severe throat infections, accompanied by loss of voice, consult a laryngologist for treatment.
7. Outrageous vocal behaviors like sighing, coughing, habitual throat clearing, yawning, belching and grunting are called "vocal hiccups."

Chapter Ten

Vocal Hygiene

The prevalence of troubled or failing voices is of epidemic,
but unrecognized proportions.
(Dr. Morton Cooper, voice and speech clinician)

Most people take better care of their SUV's, VCR's and TV's than their health. They know who to call for car repairs, what to do with electronic devices when they malfunction, where to get more memory for computer hard drives and where to go when they've caught the flu. People go to manicurists, dentists, optometrists and chiropractors on a regular basis, but few people go to an otolaryngologist for throat care.

I have included this chapter because most people do not know how to take care of their voices. More often than not, people misuse and abuse their voices everyday, and most people don't even realize they're doing it. When it comes to voice care, most people are totally unaware of the basics of vocal hygiene. Most throat problems are minor problems if they're taken care of quickly. Many *troubled* voices are caused by incorrect breathing, diet and talking habits and *not* from medical conditions like colds, post-nasal drip, and allergies.

The bottom line is once you've "found" your natural voice, it makes sense to take care of your natural voice. The good news is ninety percent of that care is up to you. It's called vocal hygiene, and that's what this chapter is about. People often come to me with voice problems they have caused! Most people fail to realize that vocal care is self-care. Taking care of your voice and keeping it in good running order just makes good business sense.

Good vocal hygiene is the difference between neglecting your voice and correcting your voice. It means settling for a voice that is not your true voice instead of enjoying your real voice (your awesome natural voice). Poor vocal habits lead to poor vocal quality. So why settle for less, when you can have so much more?

Here's how you can protect your natural voice – and your professional image from vocal toxins:

Alcohol: Alcohol is a central nervous system depressant and diuretic. It impairs motor coordination, reduces sensation and contributes to dehydration of the laryngeal mucosa. Grain alcohol, vodka and beer cause histimine reactions and create mucous. Red wines contain tannum and also increase mucous. (White wines do not produce this effect.) If you have a tendency toward phlegm, you should avoid alcohol altogether.

Caffeine: Caffeine is a diuretic (the condition that causes fluids to pass from the body without adequately hydrating the tissues). When the covers of the vocal cords become dehydrated, the phonation threshold is elevated. Because caffeine is also a stimulant, it affects the central nervous system, too. Caffeine drys the mouth and throat and can aggravate reflux (heartburn) because it weakens the lower esophageal sphincter. If you want your voice to be at its vocal best, never drink coffee immediately before you speak.

Smoking: The combination of heat and chemical irritants found in tobacco smoke cause erythema (redness due to dilation of the superficial capillaries), edema (tissue swelling), and general throat and mouth inflammation. Long-term nicotine corrosiveness can cause cellular damage which could signal the onset of chronic laryngitis, vocal cord polyps or cancer of the larynx. Smokers lose a piece of their voices with every cigarette. Smoke itself isn't the major culprit. It is the heat. Subjecting the vocal cords to 2,000-3,000 degree heat severely *fries* the exposed mucous membranes. The membranes try to protect themselves by over-secreting mucous. Thick mucous creates tissue layers on the damaged vocal cords, reddening and enlarging them. Increased mucous causes us to clear our throats which compounds the problem by stressing the vocal cords even more.

Smokeless tobacco: Chewing tobacco is more common than you think. The average age of first-time users is ten years old. Smokeless tobacco has multiple dangers and they include tooth decay, tooth loss and gum disease. Chewing tobacco contains grit and sand, which wear the enamel off teeth. Tobacco also contains sugar to improve the taste – and sugars clog the vocal cords with mucous.

Sodas and colas: Regular sodas, such as Coca-Cola, Pepsi, root beer, Dr. Pepper contain one teaspoon of sugar for every ounce of soda. A twelve-ounce can of cola, then, means drinking twelve teaspoons of sugar. This sudden sugar buzz clogs the vocal cords with mucous, which causes you to cough or clear your throat. Hacking and hurumping abuse vocal cords as well. Switch to decaffeinated diet beverages.

Drugs and medication: Cold preparations and allergy medications (antihistamines and decongestants) dry out the vocal cords. Avoid medicated sprays which cause a numbing effect on the throat since they tend to dry the throat as well.

Milk and chocolates: Chocoholics beware! Chocolates contribute to mucous build-up. Milk and other dairy products are notorious for producing mucous. Enjoy some sugar-free chocolate when you don't have to talk so much.

Dehydration: Dehydration causes the vocal fold tissues to become more viscous. Viscosity makes the tissues of the fold covers less pliable and increases phonation threshold pressure. You should drink plenty of room temperature water (8-16 glasses of water a day). Avoid drinking ice water immediately before you speak because it constricts the blood vessels around the folds. Drinking hot tea can damage the mucous membranes. I would be remiss if I recommended anything other than room temperature drinks, and that includes water and juices.

Airplanes: Airplanes are terrible environments for the vocal cords. The air quality is generally poor and dry. The beverages are usually corrosive to throats. Drink plenty of bottled water. Also avoid lengthy conversation. The ambient noise level on board is usually high and not conducive to protecting the speaking voice. I hardly ever engage in small talk with the passengers sitting next to me on planes. It's too hard on the voice. I have seen people lose their voice on a forty-five minute flight.

Restaurants: These social environments destroy more vocal cords than you would believe. They are toxic vocal environments. All of the anti-vocalization elements are there: smoke from cigarettes, alcoholic and carbonated beverages, caffeinated sodas and colas, hot drinks, chocolate and cream-filled desserts, noise and dry environments.

My best advice is to minimize talking in these environments. When you do talk, sit as close as possible to the person with whom you are speaking, and face them. In particularly noisy or toxic restaurants, amplify your voice by cupping your hands around your mouth. It's not as silly as you think it looks and it will save your voice.

Voice recognition systems: Although the jury's out on the long-term effects of voice recognition systems, the technology forces users to speak for long periods of time in an unnatural way (ie. pausing between each word). Frequent hoarseness, sore throats and temporary voice loss are some of the voice problems associated with these systems.

I recommend that whenever you use these devices that you: speak naturally, avoid whispering, breathe in through your nose, maintain good posture, keep your shoulders relaxed and slightly down, take frequent breaks and drink plenty of small sips of water. Make sure you're working in a smoke-free environment. Humidifiers help too.

Shouting or yelling: Yelling and shouting place a severe strain on the larynx and should be avoided. Use gestures or make some other kind of noise to attract someone's attention. If you attend a sporting event, whistle, clap, stomp your feet or blow a horn to show your enthusiasm. Save the vocal cords.

Clearing your throat: People who habitually have to clear their throats may have reflux disease. If you have this problem, I recommend you consult a throat specialist. For most people the best habit to follow is to sip water or swallow hard instead of clearing the throat.

You can clear your throat by coughing gently. (Ask a throat specialist to show you how.) Gentle coughs are breathy coughs. They allow you to put air through the cough instead of coughing percussively or hacking-out a cough. Gentle coughs help clear the accumulated mucous off the vocal folds, giving you the relief you seek. Sucking on glycerin lozenges can help because the glycerin soothes the vocal cords. I don't recommend menthol-coated drops because they usually irritate the vocal cords.

TMJ: TMJ (temporal mandibular joint) is the constant habit of grinding the teeth and keeping excessive tension in the jaw area adjacent to the ear. The temporal mandibular joint has fifty-six moving parts and is the most complex joint in the body. A stress-free and tension-free mandibular joint is vital to good vocal quality and production.

If you feel excess tension in your jaw, try massaging the TMJ area with your fingers, moving them in a circular motion over the joint. Sleep with your mouth gently closed instead of clinching your teeth. Massage the TMJ for four-to-five minutes several times a day. If the discomfort persists, see an otolaryngologist or your dentist.

Gastroesophageal Reflux: Gastroesophageal Reflux is caused by stomach acids that travel up the esophagus. It is commonly called heartburn. Stomach acid may spill onto the posterior region of the larynx and irritate the mucosa. This condition can become pathological. If left untreated, reflux can cause chronic throat clearing, laryngitis, hoarseness, contact ulcers (granulomas) and a host of larynx disorders.

If caught early enough and treated both medically and vocally using a speech therapist or voice coach,these ailments can be healed.

Whispering: When you whisper you use a tiny muscle located in the rear part of the larynx called the crycothyroid. It isn't a strong muscle, so it wears out quickly. When you whisper you make matters worse by exhausting an already overly-stressed muscle. So, when you are hoarse from a cold or sore throat, refrain from speaking so much and avoid whispering altogether. Rest your voice when you contract upper respiratory infections.

Fatigue: When you are tired, your voice is usually the first sign of fatigue. Vocal exhaustion generally follows physical exhaustion and is expressed as breathiness, hoarseness, dryness and tightness. Asthma and allergy sufferers must be especially careful for both vocal health and physical health reasons.

Large rooms and open spaces: In addition to voice coaching, I give keynote speeches. Oftentimes I speak to large audiences, and large audiences generally come with large rooms. That means my voice must carry from one end of the room to the other. When I speak in those circumstances, I *always* use a microphone. Proper amplification is a must. Shouting to make yourself heard or raising your voice to a higher pitch may severely damage your voice.

I also reduce the amount of my actual speaking time by inviting audience participation and using audio-visuals to support my message. I make it a practice to have a glass of room-temperature water on hand. When my audiences are especially vocal and enthusiastic, I wait to begin speaking again until they become quiet and attentive. Even if I have a microphone, I seldom raise my voice to quiet an audience. I usually can command attention by simply being silent and using effective body language.

Singing: If you sing or perform, be sure to "warm-up and cool down" your voice before and after each performance. Professional athletes always stretch before and after competitions. Voice athletes (professional speakers, trainers, consultants, singers and newscasters) know how crucial it is to take care of their voices. They know that if they lose their voice, they'll lose their career.

Here are a couple of exercises (voice aerobics) you can do to warm up your singing voice: "Yawn" from a high pitch to a low one. Repeat vowel sounds using a monotone voice. For example say: "see, see, see, knee, knee, knee, hee, hee, hee, ha, ha, ha, now, now, now ho, ho, ho;" or sing the above vowel tones on each step of the music scale using a free resonance sound. Try those for starters. Have fun with them.

Telephones: When you speak using the telephone, hold the receiver in your hand, use a shoulder rest, or purchase a head set. Never prop the receiver between your cheek and your shoulder. Contorting your neck in that fashion creates excess neck tension and affects breath support. Read this next sentence twice. *Poor posture produces a poor voice and a poor voice creates a poor professional image.* Also refrain from lying on your back during telephone conversations. The prone position reduces your breath support, making it difficult for you to vocalize adequately. Find a comfortable chair or couch to ensure proper breath support.

The problem with most people is that they do not know where to direct or how to take care of their voice.
(Dr. Morton Cooper, M.D.)

VOICE OVERS

A Summary of Points to Remember

1. People go to manicurists, dentists, optomologists and chiropractors on a regular basis, but few people go to an otolaryngologist for throat care.
2. When it comes to voice care, most people are totally unaware of vocal hygiene basics.
3. The bottom line is, once you've "found"your natural voice, it makes sense to take care of your natural voice.
4. Most people fail to realize that vocal care is self care.

(continued...)

VOICE OVERS

A Summary of Points to Remember
(continued...)

5. Taking care of your voice and keeping it in good running order is the vocal expression of who you really are.

6. Good vocal hygiene is the difference between neglecting your voice and correcting your voice.

7. The sudden sugar buzz you get from drinking regular sodas and colas clogs the vocal cords with mucous.

8. Drink 8 to 16 ounces of room temperature water every day.

9. Airplanes, noisy restaurants and large rooms are terrible environments for vocal cords.

10. Vocal exhaustion generally follows physical exhaustion.

11. When you speak in front of a large audience, always use a microphone.

12. Voice athletes (professional speakers, trainers and consultants, singers and newscasters) know how crucial it is to take care of their voices.

13. Never prop a telephone receiver between your cheek and your shoulder. It contorts your neck and creates excess vocal tension.

14. Poor posture produces a poor voice, and a poor voice creates a poor professional image.

CHAPTER ELEVEN
VOCAL AEROBICS

She was a professional athlete of the tongue. (Fannie Hurst)

Your voice is your vocal instrument. It has an infinite variety of pitch, resonance, volume and speaking rate. It works on cords and air much like musical instruments do. Once you learn to *play* it like an accomplished "vocal musician," you'll be able to coax your natural voice out of it and express the "voice" that means business anywhere, anytime.

Your own particular voice is your own special gift. The sound of your voice is one of the things that makes you so unique. It is a vocal expression of who you are. You can use your voice more effectively by nurturing it, pampering it and training it. This chapter is filled with vocal aerobics (voice exercises) for strengthening and protecting your voice. I hope you will add these aerobic workouts to your daily schedule. Most of them only take a couple of minutes, but the benefits you gain will add years to your vocal health. Use these exercises in addition to the other vocal aerobic workouts mentioned throughout this book.

> *The information most useful to me...comes from quick, and often casual verbal exchanges. This usually reaches a manager much faster than anything written down. And usually the more timely the information is, the more valuable it is.*
> *(Andrew S. Grove, CEO Intel Corp.)*

VOLUME CONTROL

Any of these vocal aerobic workouts, carried out consistently for five minutes, three or four times each day, will strengthen your support muscles and help improve your volume control. Have fun with them. They'll help you project an image of confidence and control.

TEA POT

Take a short breath. As you exhale, slowly make a hissing sound through your teeth. Maintain a gentle stream of air as you do this. h...i...s...s...s...s...s. Now hiss again, only this time count to yourself and see how long you can make the hissing last. Don't force your breath through your teeth. Send a thin stream of air out. Try it again. See if you can count up to 50, 60 or 70 before you run out of air. Be aware of your breath support. Make sure your stomach is moving in steadily as you exhale. Do not force the last breath of air out. Exhale easily and methodically.

BY THE NUMBERS

Inhale, then exhale slowly. Now take a short breath and count aloud, as fast as you can during your exhalation: 1-2-3-4-5-6-7-8-9-10-and so on. You should be able to count as high as twenty or thirty. Now count by tens as high as you can: 10-20-30-40-50-60-70-80-90-100-and so on. You should have gotten between 200 and 260.

Did you run your words together as your counted? That's okay, for the purposes of this exercise. The speed at which you were asked to count contributed to your mumbling. (This is the only time I'll ever ask you to mumble.) I'm not as concerned with how you sound as much as I am with how much breath support you maintained. Repeat this exercise a couple more times, then take a few deep, breaths and rest for a while.

NO-ING

This little gem is a very effective volume control exercise. You're probably used to hearing this particular expression. Like the rest of us you grew up on it. Say the word "no" over and over again. Start softly (almost whispering) and raise your voice slowly to a very loud, almost shouting level: "no, no, no, NO, NO." If you can't say "no" say "know." It will produce the same affect.

NAME-CALLING

What's in a name? In terms of this exercise – volumes! Begin by taking a deep breath. Inhale through your nose and exhale through your mouth. Now take a short breath and say your name softly (almost at a whisper). Repeat your name by slowly raising the volume of your voice: Linda, Linda, Linda, Linda. Do not shout your name or strain your voice. You will find your stomach contracting as if you were punched lightly in the stomach. Use the muscles in your groin, your thigh, even your buttocks. All of these muscle groups are giving your diaphragm support. Repeat this process a few times, saying your name louder each time. (If you answer yourself – enjoy your conversation.)

> *I often quote myself. It adds spice to my conversation.*
> *(George Bernard Shaw)*

PITCH NICHE

This set of exercises will help you learn to vary your pitch without straining your voice. As with all of the aerobic exercises listed in this book, be sure you are breathing properly. (See chapter 2.)

GOOD VIBRATIONS

Relax. Now take a deep breath and hold it for a count of ten. Exhale slowly. Say "aerobics" using your normal (hopefully natural) voice. Repeat it several more times without any attempt to lower your pitch. Now cup your hand over your throat and say "aerobics" again. You should feel a slight vibration in your throat. Lower your voice and say "aerobics" a few times. Lower your voice again without breathing more deeply than you did before. You should feel a strong vibration this time.

After saying "aerobics" a few more times, rest your voice You may feel some fatigue in your throat. Take a deep breath, filling both your abdomen and chest with air. Exhale and relax. Inhale slowly and then exhale, lowering your voice as you say the word "aerobics" until you've almost spent your breath. Do not force the exhalation or completely exhale. Relax. Wasn't that fun?

MARIONETTE

Sit in a kitchen or dining room chair and place both of your feet squarely on the floor, approximately twelve inches apart. Bend over from your waist toward the floor so that your chest almost touches your thighs. Your head should be dangling slightly beyond your knees and your arms should hang loosely at your sides. Your fingers should be like the limp fingers of a marionette as they touch the floor.

Relax completely. Now begin reciting a favorite poem, quote, fairy tale, nursery rhyme or prayer like: "Mary had a little lamb…" or "Row, row row your boat" or the Lord's Prayer or the Pledge of Allegiance. Your speaking voice will automatically resonate in your chest and your pitch will be lower. Listen very carefully to this sound – it's very close to the sound you want. Now straighten to a normal sitting position and repeat your recitation. Try to maintain the same voice quality you experienced in the marionette position.

> *Three things you can be judged by: your voice,*
> *your face and your disposition.*
> *(Ignas Bernstein, writer)*

RESONANCE PRESENCE

These exercises will help you establish a smooth flow of resonated air without tightening the muscles or stressing your voice.

ELBOW ROOM

Place your elbow on your desk or a table and rest your chin on the back of your hand. Your palm should be facing the desk or table top. Lift your head slightly so your chin is about two inches above the top of your hand. Say "Mah" by allowing your jaw to relax enough to touch the top of your hand. Now say "Mah, mah, mah; maw, maw, maw; mow, mow, mow" so that your jaw touches the top of your hand each time you pronounce a syllable. Place your other hand flat across your chest, just below your collarbone. Repeat the "mah, maw, mow" sequence. Do you feel the vibrations? You shouldn't have any nasality now or clinched jaw, only resonance.

KNUCKLE SANDWICH

Place the knuckle of either your index finger or middle finger between your teeth. Now read aloud a portion of this book, the Gettysburg Address, The Preamble to the United States Constitution or any other familiar passage. Read enough of the passage so you can hear yourself read. You will probably sound almost unintelligible. Now remove your knuckle sandwich and repeat your reading as you keep your jaws wide and mouth open. You should notice the resonance because you have allowed the sound – your sound – to pass through unimpeded.

HEADS UPS

Sit or stand in a comfortable position. Relax your shoulders. Let your head dangle forward so that your chin almost touches your chest. Let your head hang there and close your eyes. With your eyes closed, count slowly to ten. Count to ten again, only this time begin raising your head from its drooped position and open your eyes gradually until you see the ceiling. Repeat this drooping – lifting – drooping – lifting process a few times. You should notice your neck and shoulder tension begin to melt away.

OPEN SESAME

Hold your mouth open and say "ahhhhh." Say "ah" again, only this time yawn the "ah" out: "Ahhhhhhh." Relax and lower your shoulders as you do this. Next sound out the following word sequence by inserting your name at the proper juncture: "ahh-my-name-ahh-is-ahh-Linda-ahh." Repeat that sequence a few more times, paying particular attention to the resonate buzz around your lips and nose.

> *Oh, Lord, let my words be tender and sweet, for tomorrow I may have to eat them.*
> *(Norman Vincent Peale, minister)*

RATE HIKE

The following exercises will help you slow down so that you have better articulation and control. Although there are positive elements associated with rapid speech, speaking so fast that you don't allow someone else to speak – or allow yourself to catch your breath – creates a negative impression. Spend some time with these exercises. They'll help you slow down enough to be heard and understood.

UP SCALE

Say "do, re, mi, fa, so, la, ti, do" as fast as you can. Now emphasize "do" by saying it slowly before you race through the rest of the notes. This time slow down when you get to "re." Emphasize "mi" on your next pass and so on until you get to "do."

Now start with "do" again and go up the scale to "do." Then, without hesitating, reverse the order "do, ti, la, so, fa mi, re, do."

SHIELDS-ISMS

Read the following "Shields-isms" aloud. You will find the places to pause self-evident.

1. Your voice – comes from somewhere.
2. Have you – ever heard yourself – on a tape recording?
3. Speaking – with authority – means – sounding credible – confident – and in control.
4. Your voice – does – not – necessarily – have to age.
5. Your habitual voice – is not necessarily – your – real or natural – voice
6. Your voice – like the rest of your body – needs exercise – and – quiet time.
7. A – healthy – voice – is a – credible – voice.

'GIMME' FIVE

Say "come here" in five different ways – as if you were:
1. enticing your lover to your side;
2. speaking to a naughty child;
3. an army drill sergeant speaking to a new recruit;
4. excited about a letter you received in the mail; and
5. discovering something unexpected in the attic.

> *Some people talk because they think sound is more manageable than silence.*
> *(Margaret Halsey)*

VOICE OVERS

A Summary of Points to Remember

1. Your voice is your vocal instrument.
2. The sound of your voice is one of the things that makes you so unique.
3. You can use your voice more effectively by nurturing it, pampering it and training it.
4. Vocal exercises only take a couple of minutes, but the benefits you gain add years to your vocal health.

PART FOUR

THE VERBAL YOU

Words are the most powerful drug of (humankind).
(Rudyard Kipling)

Words are the verbal signs of ideas; vocal tones are the
signs of passions and desires. (G. W. Casper)

CHAPTER TWELVE
WORD POWER

*There are millions of words to choose from, some millions of
combinations we can use to persuade, impress, inform, entertain,
share experiences, write a scientific paper, accept a Nobel Prize,
compose a romantic novel, or leave a funny note for the paperboy.*
(Jack Thomas)

Have you ever played *Scrabble* or *Pictionary*? In
order to score well in *Scrabble*, you must be able
to use the triple letter and double word scoring blocks skill-
fully. Your ability to link words horizontally and vertically by
adding a letter or two is also helpful. Knowing how to use
words like *aardvark, abaca, azo, qat, qoph, xi* and *zax* allow
you to outscore less vocabulary-wise opponents. *Pictionary*
involves drawing pictures that represent words or phrases,
so people watching can guess what they are. Some words are
easy to draw – *house, flower, hat, book, computer*. People
without much artistic talent can draw those well enough so
other people can guess what they are. Others words like –
vocal, baffle, learning or *united* are more abstract and therefore more difficult to represent visually.

What makes these word games so enjoyable is the variety of words that can be used in a socially competitive atmosphere with mutually agreed upon rules of engagement. Both of these games give competitors ample opportunities to wow adversaries with their vocabulary mastery and analytical skill. The same communicative elements which make those games so popular are the same elements that make good conversations and speeches so informative and enjoyable. For these games to work, there must be a common language and a mutual understanding of what words mean.

When you speak, people on the receiving end of your message must be able to understand you. Effective spoken communication involves both sending and receiving clear messages. It means ensuring send-ability, receive-ability, and understand-ability, every time. It involves the vocal you, the visible you and the verbal you. It is the verbal you, the seven-to-ten percent communication part of you, that is addressed in this chapter and in the chapters which follow.

> *Never before have people had such opportunities to use their [communication] skills in responsible decision-making activities in the business environment. Never before have they had such opportunities to use them nor have they had such pressure on them to use these skills effectively and efficiently. (C. B. Stiegler, communication researcher)*

THE DICTIONARY CAN BE YOUR BEST FRIEND

Recently I coached a young manager who looked good, sounded good, but spoke poorly. He had a Southern drawl (I'll discuss drawls and accents in the next chapter) and a bad habit of misusing words. For example, in a discussion we were having over lunch about the fate of the Taliban terrorists, he referred several times to "criminal *per*secution." What he meant, of course, was "criminal *pro*secution." He also didn't differentiate between good and well. Good describes the quality of something. Well describes how something acts or performs.

Erma Bombeck is a good comedian. Erma speaks well. We discussed his misplaced word penchant, and on the walk back to his office I bought him a pocket dictionary. The lesson he learned was not to use a word unless he knew what it meant. The lesson for you is to make the dictionary your friend so you don't spoil your professional image with misplaced and mispronounced words.

> Language is not an abstract construction of the learned, or of dictionary-makers, but is something arising out of the work, needs, ties, joys, affections, tastes of generations of humanity and has its bases broad and low, close to the ground. (*Walt Whitman, poet and writer*)

PUMP UP YOUR VOCABULARY

In the preceding chapters, we've improved your visual "physique" and your vocal "musculature." Now it's time to pump up your vocabulary. Improving your vocabulary will help you go from awful to articulate. Your professional success depends on how well you speak and how well you speak depends on how intelligent you sound.

If you don't know the meaning of or how to pronounce the following words, I recommend your spending some quality time building your vocabulary:

apropos	minutiae
beguile	panache
brevity	paradigm
camaraderie	prerogative
entrepreneur	quixotic
forte	savoir faire
hyperbole	taut
insouciant	umbrage
irascible	vignette
liaison	visceral
milieu	zealous

One final comment to tuck away in your *FYI Bank*: It is ironic that one of the most commonly mispronounced words in the English language is – pronunciation.

> *Long sentences in a short composition are like large rooms in a little house.*
> *(William Shenstone)*

BUMPER STICKER PHRASES

Have you noticed how the media loves sound-bytes? The media quotes some celebrities, sports people and influential authorities more than others who are just as famous. Radio talk shows invite certain people back more than others. Part of the recurrent interest is subject matter, but a great deal of the interest is due to the individual's command of the English language and his or her ability to "wow" the audience with a one-liner or phrase terms differently than anyone else. I call these memorable sound-bytes "bumper sticker phrases."

One of the benefits of word power is knowing enough words so you can link them together in a novel, memorable way. For example, catch phrases like – "to err is human," "the hurrier I go, the behinder I get," "the medium is the message," "buy low, sell high," "make love, not war," "ready, aim, fire," "crazy like a fox," "if you snooze, you lose," – are all well-known expressions.

If you want to be memorable, if you want to get quoted by colleagues and friends, if you want to be viewed as someone who can think creatively on your feet, develop a few bumper sticker phrases of your own. Learn how to turn a good phrase or insert a neat word to amplify your message.

> *Wit is the salt of conversation, not the food.*
> *(William Hazlitt)*

TATTERED WORDS

English is an incredibly rich language. There are so many different ways to say everything. Good communicators stay current by adopting new expressions to replace old, worn-out words and phrases. Over-used words and phrases crop up in every conversation and affect the over-all impression people have of each other. I have listed below some of the most hackneyed words and phrases I have heard my clients

use. They are commonly-used expressions, but I recommend
your not using them in formal or business settings:

As a matter of fact...	Let's face it...
At any rate...	No problem...
And stuff like that...	Right on!
And whatnot...	Say, listen...
Do yo know what I mean?	Say what...
Get outta here...	So to speak...
I'll be honest with you...	Whatever...
It goes without saying...	Yeah...
It's a cinch...	You've got to be kidding...
Is that right?	You don't say...

Although these phrases can show your attentiveness
and support, they become irritating when they're over-used.
If you over-use any of these expressions, adopt a more up-
to-date expression to add variety to your responses.

> *We do not live by words alone, despite the fact*
> *that sometimes we have to eat them.*
> *(Adlai Stevenson)*

WORD WARPS

I call misused words and phrases "word warps." They
are the type of words that leave negative impressions and are
not the kind of things you want to say in front of anyone,
especially colleagues and customers. For example, the infamous
"ain't" is one of the most commonly-used expressions in
America. It's the contraction of *are* and *not* and *am* and *not*:
"I ain't doin' so good," or "she ain't my type." The contraction
"aren't" is the accepted version and should be used during
business conversations.

Two more undignified "warps" which flout the English language every time they're uttered are "hisself" and "theirself." The appropriate words for each are "himself" and "themselves" respectively. Adding an "s" to the end of anywhere (anywheres), nowhere (nowheres), somewhere (somewheres), and anywhere (anywheres) warps their use, making the person who misspoke seem uneducated. They are horrible word warps which should be deleted from the English language.

> *The meaning of words changes so dramatically that today's slang may be obsolete tomorrow.*
> *(Lillian Glass, author)*

EMOTIONALLY CHARGED WORDS

We'd all like to think that we're rational human beings, capable of self-control and forgiveness, especially when it comes to fielding a nasty comment from someone. We've all heard the old maxim, "sticks and stones may break my bones, but words will never hurt me." Most us of grew up on that incantation. I incorporated it into my vocal repertoire by the time I was three years old. It came in handy when I dealt with the slights or nitpicking tossed at me by my kinder-care playmates. You probably had similar experiences as a child.

As we grow into adulthood, we discover that certain words *can* hurt, and they can hurt very much. And when they hurt, people get defensive and angry. Water boils at 212° F. It boils every time at its "boiling point." People have boiling points, too, but unlike water, people boil at different temperatures. And those temperatures generally come as emotionally charged words.

Inflammatory words will heat up any conversation or meeting. Using derogatory, sexist and fascist language creates enemies and infuriates people. Avoid words that demean and insult people. Disparaging remarks cause people to have a low opinion of you. Refuse to use words that bait people, that create hostilities, that wreak havoc with people's emotions. Words are powerful things. They can be used to injure people or inspire them, cause grudges that cut or craft relationships, create friends or make enemies.

While words have definitions, they also have meanings, and those meanings are usually either denotative or connotative. Their denotative meanings are usually dictionary meanings, which keep them objective, precise and literal. For example, the dictionary (denotative) meaning of *school* is a "place or institution of educational discipline, a building where educational instruction takes place, a place of learning." Its connotative meaning is much more interpretative and variable, because connotation includes all the feelings, associations and emotions the word touches off in different people.

It is the emotional component attached to words which electrifies those words, making them highly charged statements. Using the word *school* as an example again, some people associate *schools* with personal growth, childhood friendships that blossomed into life-long relationships, proms and a few special teachers that made the school years worthwhile. For others, *school* may have been a frustrating, unfulfilling and boring experience.

Powerful words usually result in powerful reactions. Choose your words wisely. Become more aware of the difference between their denotative and connotative meanings. It's usually the connotative meanings associated with words that create the sparks and turn seemingly innocent words into emotionally charged verbal exchanges.

> *We (could) have…many fewer disputes in the world if words were taken for what they are, the signs of our ideas, and not for things themselves.*
> *(John Locke)*

YOUR VERBAL RESUMÉ

Every time you speak, you are up-dating your verbal resumé. Every word, every inflection, every pause is judged by others. Words can indicate what kind of person you are, your likes and dislikes, your character or lack of character. They can tell how much education you have, how confident or guarded you are, how out-going or shy you are. People can sense what it would be like to work with you, to trust you, to depend on you, to co-chair a project with you.

People remember what you say, and how you said it. When you speak, people decide whether or not they like you, respect you or admire you. Words are your verbal tools. They can build your credibility or destroy it, enhance your professional image or ruin it. There's so much power in your words that you can leave people speechless or cause them to speak out against you. You can win customers or wound customers, infuriate co-workers or invigorate co-workers.

Although the spoken word only amounts to seven percent of your business communication worth, words can be assets or liabilities. To fulfill their basic function as communication devices, words must be understandable, intelligible, articulate and accurate to "spruce up" your verbal resumé. Nothing is more irritating to listeners than a speaker's nervousness, self-consciousness and inability to articulate vowels and consonants accurately and meaningfully.

Your paper resumé may look terrific. Your experience and employment history may look good on paper. Your physical appearance and referrals may be impeccable. But oftentimes your verbal resumé can sabotage your success if you can't craft the spoken word as succinctly and as power-fully as the written word.

The pen is the tongue of the mind.
(Miguel de Cervanes-Saavedra)

No member needs so great a number of muscles as the tongue; this exceeds all the rest in the number of its movements.
(Leonardo da Vinci, artist & sculptor)

I'll discuss anything. I like to go perhaps-ing around on all subjects.
(Robert Frost, writer & poet)

VOICE OVERS

A Summary of Points to Remember

1. Effective spoken communication means ensuring send-ability, receive-ability and understand-ability every time.
2. Make the dictionary your friend so you don't spoil your professional image with misplaced and mispronounced words.
3. Pump up your vocabulary so you can go from awful to articulate.
4. Develop a few "bumper sticker phrases" so you can wow listeners with a memorable comment or two.
5. Misused words like hisself, theirself and ain't are "word warps." They leave negative impressions and make you appear uneducated.
6. Refuse to use words that demean and insult people, words that bait people, that create hostilities, that wreak havoc with people's emotions.
7. It is the connotative (emotional) meaning, not the denotative (dictionary) meaning, of words that make them electrically charged.
8. The spoken word is your verbal resumé.

CHAPTER THIRTEEN
VERBAL HICCUPS

"Everybody says words different," says Ivy. "Arkansas folks says 'em different, and Oklahomy folks says 'em different. And we seen a lady from Massachesetts, an' she say 'em differentest of all. Couldn't hardly make out what she was sayin'". (John Steinbeck in The Grapes of Wrath)

Generally speaking, we Americans are not quite as articulate as our British friends and colleagues. Our diction isn't as crisp and our word pronunciations are sloppy. Most Americans have never had a speech lesson or oral interpretation class, let alone voice coaching. Diction, enunciation and articulation classes aren't high priorities in educational settings or business training seminars. But all of this is changing. Corporate America is waking up to the harsh realities of sloppy enunciation, faulty diction and poor articulation.

Businesses are becoming much more image-conscious. They are concerned about the performance of their products, the way customers are served, and how well their customer-contact people *communicate* with both internal and external customers. Companies want language barriers eliminated. They want employees who can articulate the benefits of their products and services. One company executive told me, "Linda, I tell my salespeople I don't want prices or language to get in the way of an important sale. What good does it do if my people know the product, but can't articulate the product?"

I call verbal misfires like mispronunciation, poor articulation and diction, slang, heavy accents, jargon, fillers (ums, uhs, and ahs) wordiness and profanity "verbal hiccups." They have no place in your business vocabulary. In some cases they can be career-stoppers. So if you have serious aspirations as a manager, speaker, consultant or trainer, you should develop a plan to improve your speaking ability. This book is a good start. However, if you really want to excel as someone who is a consummate communicator, I highly recommend your adding a voice coach to your personal/professional development team.

Let's talk briefly about the kinds of "verbal hiccups" that can wreck your career. Some of them may seem obvious. Others may surprise you. But all of them will tarnish your verbal resumé and dampen the prospects of your presenting the kind of professional image you want. It may seem obvious that presenting a good verbal impression is the right impression, but you would be amazed at the number of people who clutter their conversation with "ums," "uhs," jargon and slang.

Rhetoric is the art of ruling (people's) minds. (Plato)

158

POOR DICTION, ENUNCIATION AND ARTICULATION

Sloppy enunciation, questionable articulation and poor diction give listeners the impression that the speaker is uneducated, unskilled and incompetent. Using language correctly involves three key elements: enunciation, diction and articulation.

Articulation means using your "articulators" (lips, tongue, teeth, lower jaw, upper gums, palate and throat) to form a sound. Good articulation means keeping your articulators relaxed and flexible when you speak. *Diction* is the total production of your sounds. You can be *lip lazy*, sloppy or crisp. One of my coaching clients used to say "off-ten" for "often" and "list'nin" for "listening." Enunciation is the way words are delivered, and in particular, where accents are placed.

Since diction is governed by your lips, teeth and tongue, your lips should hit slightly against each other on the *p, b, and m* sounds; lips are rounded for the *w* and *wh* sounds. Try this simple diction exercise: Say "papa" slowly seven times. Next say "mama" seven times. Then say, "baba" seven times. Make sure your lips touch as you sound out the words. Now say all three words consecutively as fast as you can without becoming sloppy in your enunciation, "papa, mama, baba – papa, mama, baba."

One of my clients used to say "he kep it" for "he kept it." He also had a small lisp, which we corrected. He used to say "mah thithter," instead of "my sister." His sloppy enunciation was compounded by poor articulation as well. People who enunciate poorly usually mispronounce "ing" at the end of words (goin', doin', comin', instead of go*ing*, do*ing*, and com*ing*). People mispronounce words for many reasons. Some people have nervous problems. Others have poor hygiene issues which affect the way they move their articulators. Still others have spaces between teeth, missing teeth, protruding teeth, poor fitting dentures and new crowns that contribute to poor pronunciation. Most people mispronounce words because they are lip lazy.

Most people have difficulty pronouncing certain types of sounds called *plosive* (air-producing sounds: *p, t, k, b, d,* and *g*), *fricative* (noise-producing sounds: *f, v, ch, j, zh, sh, s* and *z*), *nasal sounds* (*m, n, ng*) and gliding sounds (*l* and *r*).

Try the following exercises to sharpen your articulation and enunciation:

Say these sounds as fast as you can: *pppp, bbbb, tttt, dddd, kkkk, gggg.*

Say each sentence as fast as you can:
1. Place the plate properly.
2. Buy Buddy a blue bun.
3. Tim, the tall tattered tinker, sat.
4. Didn't you dupe the dope?
5. Kiss the kindly kitty cat quickly.
6. Glaring gladly at the golf glass.

Say each of these sounds as fast as you can in succession: *ffff, vvvv, ch, ch, ch, ch, jjjj, zh, zh, zh, zh, sh, sh, sh, sh, ssss, zzzz.* Now repeat these sounds in **reverse order** as fast as you can.

Say these twenty "m's as fast as you can: *mmm mmmmmmmmmmmmmmmmmmm.* Now fly through these: *mmmmm, nnnnn, ngngngngng.*

Those exercises are a good start. I recommend your working with a voice coach to develop a program for your improvement. Meanwhile, I encourage you to have some fun with these.

> *There can be no fairer ambition*
> *than to excel in talk.*
> (Robert Louis Stevenson)

SLANG

Every generation has its slang. Sometimes a generation is defined by its slang. Interestingly enough, average adults have approximately 10,000 to 12,000 words in their vocabulary. Most people use only ten-to-twenty percent of that vocabulary. Of that small percentage, a little over three percent of the words spoken are slang. Isn't that interesting!

Remember when the word "cool" meant the opposite of warm, a "fox" was a four-legged forest animal, and "stoked" described what you did to a fire place? We have made an industry out of slang. There are mountain bike slang dictionaries, rap dictionaries, business buzzword dictionaries, nonsense dictionaries called nonsensicons, and limerick dictionaries. *Ace's* used to be cards, now we have *ace* reporters or people who *ace* exams. *Antifreeze* is the fluid used to protect car radiators from freezing, but it also stands for liquor or coffee which warms the blood on cold days. *Armpit* refers to the body, but it also means an undesirable place. *Zip* meant fast, but today it means ignorance: "He knows zip about voice awareness." More recently we have slang expressions like: couch potato (TV groupie), crib (home), flick (movie), meltdown (fatigue), nuke (microwave food), veg out (relax or loaf), scarf (eat food) and so on.

Although American businesses have "chilled out" in terms of dress codes, work schedules, home offices as well as the use of slang, most supervisory and upper level management positions frown on the heavy use of slang. Slang can add a certain vividness to a business conversation, but it can offend or baffle customers and colleagues alike. It's best to limit your use of slang unless you work in an environment that accepts a certain amount of slang infestation.

> *What was a "jerk" four years ago is a "nerd" by today's standards. What was "swell" in the fifties, "groovy" in the sixties, and "hot" in the seventies, is "incredible" in the eighties. (Lillian Glass, author)*

HEAVY DIALECTS, DRAWLS AND ACCENTS

Cultural and regional dialects, drawls and accents are charming reminders that each of us is a unique multi-faceted individual, and that our background is reflected, at least partially, in our speech patterns. People ask me all the time if they need to "ditch" their accents. I almost always say, "No, accents are part of who you are. They're part of what makes you so special."

While watching the events and the aftermath of the terrorists attacks on the World Trade Center and the Pentagon, I was moved by all of the interviews I saw with family members of the victims. The cultural diversity was awesome. The victims of those attacks were from cultures all over the world. I was moved by each family member's story and felt an emotional bond, despite hearing their foreign accents. All three major networks, including CNN and FOX gave us the impression that we were one people and that our ethnic and cultural diversity didn't matter. How we spoke didn't matter either. We were all Americans, united by the tragic events and united by common bonds of love, caring and decency.

September eleventh has passed and most people are recovering emotionally, financially and spiritually. They are becoming their "pre-nine-eleven" selves again. They are expressing their old prejudiced selves, judging people by the way they look and by the way they talk. For example, although many Americans find a Southern drawl charming, tourists from Georgia or North Carolina had better not drawl out their southern vowels too long if they're asking for directions in Boston, Newark or New York City. By the same token, barking out your need for directions using a Bronx or Brooklyn accent while you're vacationing in Biloxi, Mississippi or Charleston, South Carolina may offend the locals.

Accents have one thing in common: they mean you are from somewhere else other than from here. Unfortunately, people harbor prejudices against people who sound differently, dress differently and act differently. Personally, I love to hear people with accents. I love to hear the rich Latin accent of Antonio Banderas, and Dolly Parton's sweet, Southern, Tennessee drawl is endearing. So, what drawls, dialects and accents do people like or dislike in the United States? In a study conducted by Dr. Lillian Glass and published in her book *Talk to Win*, she recorded the reactions people had to thirty different accents. They rated the accents from the best liked to the least liked. Her results are listed below:

Most Liked Accents	Least Liked Accents
Australian	Arabic
English	Black English
Irish	Brooklyn
Italian	Chinese
Greek	Iranian
French	Korean
Jamaican	Russian
Southern	German
South African	Vietnamese

The accents that were rated low had two things in common: they were all hard to understand and there were significant vocal biases and prejudices associated with that particular nationality. I am not suggesting that you abandon your cultural and ethnic heritage. However, if you have a heavy accent, one that has negative stereotypes associated with it, you may want to modify it enough to negate the unfavorable cultural biases attached to it.

> *A fine German accent may bolster a psychiatrist's fee. A crisp British accent simply cries for a lecture tour...To speak as they do in Dixie – as long as it is intelligible – is a sentimental plus. The New England twang conjures up visions of democracy in the raw...But (out-of-town New Yorkers) abominate the New York accent.*
> *(Richard Shepard)*

JARGON

Some people use jargon to show superiority. Others use it to confuse people to protect their turf or prevent people from becoming part of the "clique." In most organizations, jargon is used to shorten the names of work processes and technical applications. Unfortunately for anyone outside the "group" jargon creates a communication barrier. Jargon comes from technical manuals, papers and textbooks associated with a particular discipline. Every industry has its jargon. Engineers have it. Computer hackers and accountants use it proudly. Management, human resources, marketing and sales organizations have their own idiosyncratic jargon. Even families have their "insider" language.

Although jargon allows "insiders" to communicate quite well with each other, it creates a barrier for "outsiders" who are not privy to its subtle nuances and technical implications. For example, the term "ambush marketing" sounds clever and exciting, but what does it mean? It refers to the practice of tying a firm's name to its competitors advertising to reap marketing benefits.

Let's try several more technical neologisms to demonstrate how vague – and interesting – they can be. What is a "dancing frog" as it applies to computers? It's a problem that occurs when the user is trying to get some work done, but fails to appear when the technician arrives. The term was first popularized by Warner Brothers in the cartoon "One Froggy Evening" which featured a dancing and singing Michigan J. Frog that simply croaked when anyone else was around.

Most people can identify with the techno-phrase "like nailing jelly to a tree," but what does it mean? It is computer hacker jargon for describing tasks thought to be impossible, especially those in which the difficulties arise from poor specifications or the inherent slipperiness within the problem domain. Here's a couple from my profession. What's a "voice-net"? It's a telephone. How about a "voice." It means to phone someone instead of e-mailing them: "I'm busy now, give me time to get my ducks in a row (another piece of jargon) and I'll *voice* you later." "Stir-fried random" is jargon for workaholics who fry fresh vegetables and meat or reheat left-overs in woks. "Spam" is a meat product but it also stands for receiving unwanted truck-loads of email. "Bandaids" cover cuts and scratches, but in jargonize they stand for quick fixes to business problems which usually require permanent solutions later.

Jargon, in and of itself, isn't a terrible communications tool. It can be a very effective tool if it isn't over-used or used indiscriminately as a secret language for the privileged few. I recommend economical use of jargon in "mixed" company and when it is used, it should be explained to newcomers so they, too, can enjoy techno-speak.

> *We all know that the preferred term is "correctional facility" instead of prison. But did you know that now it's "behavior adjustment unit (BAU)" for short, instead of solitary confinement? (KYW-TV)*

UMS, UHS, AND AHS

For some curious reason, people seem to be uncomfortable with silence. So they *fill* pauses in conversation with interjections like *um, uh,* and *ah, you know, whatever* and *fuhget about it.* We all do it. We want to show interest and take part in conversations so we fill in conversational gaps with sound. Unfortunately, these interjections can detract from the message. They are the verbal equivalent of grunts. They are styrofoam words which fill in the silent spaces around conversation.

Recently, one of my coaching clients asked me to help, well, *you know,* rid him of, *you know,* his, *you know* problem. He was addicted to the "you know" phrase. He used it in almost every sentence he spoke. Early on in our coaching partnership, I counted the number of times he used "you know" during a fifteen minute conversation. He said you know seventy-six times – that' a little over five times a minute. I found myself side-tracked by his cavalcade of "you knows" to such an extent that I was unaware of almost everything else he said.

Cluttering his conversation with so many "you knows" made him appear unintelligent, less confident and certainly less assertive and competent. His "you know" habit raised questions about his promotability, too, since people thought he was stalling or didn't know the answers to technical questions. He was quite bright, but his "vocal styrofoam" habit was killing him.

Monitor your own use of filler words. Tape record yourself as you talk on the phone to family members and friends, or record one of your favorite vacation stories by speaking into a microphone in the privacy of your office or home. Play back the tape and notice how frequently you use filler words. "Ask your family or closest friends to help you kick the habit by reminding you every time you use a filler word. Once you become aware of your filler problem, you'll be able to stop yourself with a little help from your friends.

> *Nothing words, like "um," "ah," and "you know" are oral crutches. They are handy to lean on when you're stalling, but if you get dependent on them, your conversation will always limp along. (Larry King, CNN talk show host)*

WORDINESS

In the concise and precise business world, communication wordiness shortens careers. The maxim "time is money" applies to communication as much as it does work processes, engineering and distribution. Unnecessary words and redundancy are the chief causes of wordiness. Your business voice will be stronger and you will sound more articulate if you shorten your sentences. For example, compare the two columns below:

Wordiness	Conciseness
in the event that	if
was able to obtain	got
having pondered and consid-	
ered the options	decided
finally come about	happened

The word usage on the right is preferred both conversationally and in writing. Being redundant is another matter. Some people, it seems, believe two words are better than one, like an *aching headache* or *considerable fortune.* The modifiers aching and considerable are unnecessary since headache and fortune speak for themselves. In the following sentences, the italicized words should be omitted: a *completely* bankrupt company; an *incredibly* unbelievable turn of events; a *hot* race car; an *extremely* verbose speaker.

Can you identify the popular versions of the following phrases? (The answers are at the end of this segment.)

1. A pair offers the possibility of companionship, while triploideaties considered as an aggregate assume overpowering characteristics of a multitude.

2. Lavation is in proximity to a state of piety.

3. The art of combining vocal or instrumental sounds or tones in varying melody, harmony, rhythm and timbre in order to form structurally complete, expressive composition mollifies the uncultured primitive.

Wordiness is tiresome to the listener, lessens the credibility and effectiveness of the speaker, and pollutes the message with unnecessary verbage. Less is more when you communicate in business settings. Use the KISS technique: **Keep It Short and Simple.**

If you're on the receiving end of someone's long-windedness, there are several tactics you can use to bring the speaker back to his/her point or to end the conversation. If a long-winded person asks to speak to you, limit the time by putting him/her on notice by saying, "Yes, I have a minute or two before I have to …" or "I can give you a couple of minutes, but then I have to…" or simply refuse by saying, "You've caught me at a bad time. I can see you at such and such a time for a few minutes between meetings."

When you're engaged in conversations with "motor mouths," you can always interrupt their tiresome monologues by asking questions that require one-word answers or asking them tactfully to get to the point. Sometimes you've just got to be assertive and stop the conversation by saying, "I'm, sorry" or "time out – I didn't realize this was going to be so involved. We'll need to chat later." Most people listen politely to a motor mouth. Unfortunately, allowing motor mouths the opportunity to filibuster you for the next twenty or thirty minutes or longer, only encourages them.

Answers to phrases:
1. Two's company, three's a crowd.
2. Cleanliness is next to Godliness.
3. Music soothes the savage beast.

I don't care how much a man talks, if he only says it in a few words. (Josh Billings)

PROFANITY

As liberal as we 21st Century Americans think we are, most people are still offended by someone who curses or swears. Although the increased use of profanity in both business and social settings seems more acceptable today, most people are annoyed by it. Four-lettered words still carry a stigma. We view people who use them as uncouth, rebellious and offensive. There's something about the way a profane word sounds that makes people uncomfortable.

People who habitually use profanity are judged to be less sociable, less intelligent, less credible, less approachable and less attractive than someone who doesn't swear. While profanity rubs most people the wrong way, occasionally it rubs *off* on some people. You've probably noticed how some conversations degenerate once someone uses profanity. Like any other bad habit, people can get used to it – and habits are hard to break.

If you swear and want to curb your swearing habit – or someone else's –there are several things you can do. Use a tactic similar to eliminating the use of filler words or slang. Monitor your use of profanity. Tape record yourself. Ask trusted friends and colleagues to remind you when you curse. Make a list of substitute words you can use instead of curse words. Practice using them so you can build more acceptable words into your vocabulary.

Sixty years ago America gasped when Rhett Butler told Scarlett O'Hara at the end of Gone With the Wind, "Frankly, my dear, I don't give a damn." Profanity on the silver screen was unthinkable. Today, unless we limit our viewing to Walt Disney Cartoons and the Nickelodeon Channel, we are exposed to a level of profanity that our parents would have found unacceptable. (Jo-Ellen Dimitrius, Ph.D. author)

VOICE OVERS

A Summary of Points to Remember

1. Unfortunately, diction, enunciation and articulation classes aren't high priorities in educational settings or business training seminars.
2. Sloppy pronunciation, questionable articulation and poor diction give listeners the impression that the speaker is uneducated, unskilled and incompetent.
4. Every generation has its slang, and sometimes a generation is defined by its slang.
5. Cultural and regional dialects, drawls and accents are charming reminders that each of us is a unique, multi-faceted individual.
6. Use the KISS technique: Keep it short and simple.
7. Four-letter words still carry a stigma. We view people who use them as uncouth, rebellious and offensive.

CHAPTER FOURTEEN

LISTENING: DEVELOPING YOUR EAR-ABILITY

Two men were walking down a crowded sidewalk in a downtown business area. Suddenly one exclaimed: "Listen to the lovely sound of that cricket." But the other could not hear. He asked his companion how he could detect the sound of a cricket amidst the din of people and traffic. The first man, who was a zoologist, had trained himself to listen to the voices of nature, but he did not explain. He simply took a coin out of his pocket and dropped it on the sidewalk, whereupon dozens of people began to look about them. "We hear," he said, "what we want to hear."
(Bhagwan Shree Rajneesh)

The famous novelist and philosopher, André Gide, began one of his lectures by saying, "All this has been said before, but since nobody listened, it must be said again." I have included a chapter on listening because it is the other half of speaking. Without effective listening, speaking would fall on deaf ears. So many things we hear go in one ear and out the other. When we hear something for the first time, we usually remember only half of what we hear. Two days later, we've forgotten half of that. Our inability to remember what we *hear* is directly related to our inability to *listen* attentively.

Let's take a look at the distinction between hearing and listening. According to Webster's *New World Dictionary*, listening is the "ability to make a conscious, purposeful effort to hear" or "to pay attention to what is heard." Hearing is the "sense by which sound is perceived by the ear." Hearing, then, involves the physiological reception of sound, while listening applies to the perception of meaningful sound. Hearing is an automatic physiological reaction of the senses and nervous system to the sounds we hear. Listening is an attitude, a voluntary psychological response to the sounds we choose to hear.

We hear hundreds of sounds each minute, but we listen to only a select few sounds, the sounds we label both consciously and subconsciously as relevant to our health, safety and well-being. We block out other sounds. For example, when you are concentrating on an important project at work, you ignore the conversations of nearby co-workers, phones chiming in adjacent cubicles, footsteps of busy-co-workers trailing down the aisleway, and so on. New employees may be bothered by all of the office noise until they become more familiar with the hustle and bustle. Similarly, people who live in the suburbs ignore the sound of crickets and chorus of birds, while city people become fascinated by the plethora of natural sounds. In both cases, people notice unfamiliar sounds and ignore familiar, common place sounds.

People may adapt to noise but they pay attention to valuable information. Noise is considered unpleasant, obnoxious sounds. Meaningful information gets our attention because it is considered interesting, relevant and life-supporting. Prolonged exposure to noise, whether it's the rat-tat-tat of jack hammers and car horns or the boring, monotonous tone of the motor mouth trying to monopolize a conversation, is an upsetting experience which sends listeners running for cover.

Listening is the sensory channel used most often for learning. As I've described above, most people assume listening and hearing are the same thing. That is an unfortunate misconception because it leads us to believe listening, like hearing, is instinctive. As a result most people fail to develop their listening skills and deny themselves countless opportunities to "hear the crickets."

The audible you is just as important as the vocal you, the verbal you and the visual you. It demands your energy, commitment and discipline. Listening, like proper vocalization, is a learned skill – and an attitude. It is an active, not a passive process. You can become a better listener if you want to become a better listener, and you will become a better speaker when you practice listening. You begin to move others, to influence them, to validate them, to gain their trust and respect the moment you develop your ear-ability.

Speaking is a (partnership) between the talker and the listener against the forces of confusion. Unless both make the effort, interpersonal communications is quite hopeless.
(Norbert Weiner, author)

HOW'S YOUR EAR-ABILITY?

Let's take a quick look at the audible you. Complete the following listening self-evaluation by checking the appropriate box to the right of the ear-ability characteristic that best describes your listening ability:

Ear-ability Self-Test

Ear-ability Characteristic	Mostly	Occasionally	Rarely
1. I make good eye contact with the person talking.	☐	☐	☐
2. I think about some kind of rebuttal while the other person is talking.	☐	☐	☐
3. I learn something from everyone I meet	☐	☐	☐
4. I practice active listening techniques.	☐	☐	☐
5. I tune out people if they say something I don't want to hear.	☐	☐	☐
6. I can control myself when I hear emotionally-charged words.	☐	☐	☐
7. The "ums, uhs, and ahs" people use during conversations affect the quality of my listening.	☐	☐	☐
8. I daydream during conversations.	☐	☐	☐
9. I look up definitions to words I hear that are unfamiliar to me.	☐	☐	☐
10. I listen attentively to other people's new points even if they're different from mine.	☐	☐	☐
11. I can listen to accents, dialects and drawls without being distracted by them.	☐	☐	☐
12. I can restate instructions and messages accurately to show I understand what was said.	☐	☐	☐
13. I can listen to someone's profanity or slang without becoming defensive.	☐	☐	☐
14. I pay attention to what is being said even though I'm not interested.	☐	☐	☐
15. I can finish someone's sentence.	☐	☐	☐
16. I can give the appearance of listening even when I'm not.	☐	☐	☐
17. I interrupt people when they talk.	☐	☐	☐

Ear-ability Characteristic	Mostly	Occasionally	Rarely
18. I take notes so I can remember what someone says.	☐	☐	☐
19. I can listen to a wordy person without becoming impatient.	☐	☐	☐
20. I judge people by the way they talk.	☐	☐	☐

Scoring Index: Find the box you checked in each column and match your response with the number assigned to that response. Circle your responses below. Count the number of circles down each column and write the total for each column on the line below that column:

	Mostly	Occasionally	Rarely
1.	3	2	1
2.	1	2	3
3.	3	2	1
4.	3	2	1
5.	1	2	3
6.	3	2	1
7.	1	2	3
8.	1	2	3
9.	3	2	1
10.	3	2	1
11.	3	2	1
12.	3	2	1
13.	3	2	1
14.	3	2	1
15.	1	2	3
16.	1	2	3
17.	1	2	3
18.	3	2	1
19.	1	2	3
20.	1	2	3
Total:	_____	_____	_____

Ear-ability Score:
> 55 to 60 (Excellent);
> 48 to 54 (Good);
> 40 to 47 (Average);
> 39 and below (Poor).

Now stop for just a minute. List all of the sounds you hear in 60 seconds. Do this two or three times a day in different environments over the next three days. Build these "listening retreats" into your overall business voice development plan. You will notice a definite improvement in your "ear-ability."

> *If people are unwilling to hear you, you had better hold your tongue. (Earl of Chesterfield)*

WHY WE DON'T LISTEN

Our attitudes toward listening began in childhood. The infant equivalent of listening is lying wide-eyed in the crib, moving his or her little head from side-to-side, and blinking amazement at the sounds in the room. All of these actions, of course, get little attention from the parents. Crying, the infant equivalent of speaking, is usually accompanied by the flailing of tiny arms and legs and immediate attention from concerned parents who pick the child up and give it all kinds of attention. Even negative attention (anger or frustration from care givers) is better than no attention. Infants learn a very important lesson early on in life: talking (raising the decibel level of their cries and pouts) is rewarded more than listening (quietly observing the world around them). That message is repeated throughout childhood and reinforced significantly in adulthood.

How often do you remember hearing these expressions?:
"Don't interrupt me when I'm talking."
"Look at me when I'm talking to you."
"Don't speak until you're spoken to."
"Shut-up" or "shut-up and listen."
"Don't talk back."
"I'm going to count to three."
"Listen to me."

A child who hears these caustic messages feels threatened and uneasy, and this discomfort becomes associated with listening. Messages like the ones listed above create negative thoughts and plant seeds of resistance in the child's mind against listening. For example, a child who is repeatedly told to "shut-up" or is constantly threatened with "shut-up and listen" may counter by responding "I won't shut-up. I won't listen, and nobody's gonna make me." A child growing up in that kind of negative environment will probably grow up with an embattered self-image *and* poor listening skills, as well as other anti-social attitudes and behaviors.

There are any number of reasons why people fail to listen properly or simply refuse to listen. People generally speak at the rate of 140-190 words per minute. Listeners can process information at around 350-500 words per minute. People spend this "extra" time going on mental vacations, daydreaming or thinking about what they want to say next.

The chief reasons people experience "hearing loss" are outlined below. Most people, according to researchers, Thomas Gordon, Isaac Rubin, and Robert Bolton, refuse to listen when they are:

- threatened or issued a harsh warning;
- ordered or directed to do something;
- criticized, blamed, shamed or humiliated;
- disagreed with by someone they feel is inferior;
- told what they should do or ought to do;

- lectured at or argued with;
- cursed at or called a demeaning name;
- severely questioned or interrogated;
- angry or withdrawn;
- zealously counseling or coaching someone;
- sure they don't need advice;
- feeling over-confident and pompous

Unfortunately many of these anti-listening behaviors occur just as much at work as they do in social settings. The short list of costs associated with faulty listening at work include missed project deadlines, botched customer service, duplication of work, repeated mistakes, lack of strategic direction, lost customers, redundant paperwork and customer complaints.

The good news is once you know why people don't listen, you can remove the roadblocks to good listening and replace them with open, honest, results-oriented communication. That whole clarification process requires an understanding of the socialization process. It must take into account such "filters" as beliefs, values, assumptions, attitudes, expectations, prejudices, interests and feelings. All of us listen through these filters. Good listeners understand how these filters shape listening behavior and devise ways to counteract their negative effects.

> *Your ear keeps your foot out of your mouth.*
> *(Sam Deep, consultant and speaker)*

USE YOUR HEARING AIDS

Good listening is everyone's business, and good business is listening to everyone. That's about as succinctly as I can put it. Listening to customers, heeding market trends, eavesdropping on hungry competitors, keeping customers' needs within earshot, tapping into customers' expectations, and bending an ear to hear colleagues' innovative ideas are all sound listening strategies. And they can be learned! The following listening techniques will pump up your ear-ability.

1. **Decide that you really want to listen:** Preoccupy yourself with listening. Buy books on listening (this chapter is a good start). Attend seminars on effective listening. Practice listening. Earlier in this chapter, I asked you to list all of the sounds you heard in 60 seconds. Try it again. Right now. For the next minute list all of the sounds you hear – including the sound of your pencil or pen against your notepaper. Try it again just before you go to sleep tonight.

2. **Learn to block out competing thoughts and sounds:** Remember, your ears work twice as fast and your mind works five times as fast as the average person can speak. So, fight the temptation to wander off.

3. **Listen with an ear for learning:** Good listeners expect to learn something because they listen for something. They concentrate on what's said because they want to remember what's said.

4. **Give people a chance to finish their sentence:** Anytime you interrupt people and keep them from finishing their thoughts, you risk irritating them. According to most listening research polls, being interrupted is the number one complaint people have when they're trying to get their message across.

5. **Listen to what others say about themselves:** Get on their wavelength. Hear the hidden messages behind the words. Indicate how much you want to hear what they have

to offer, whether you are speaking to the President of the United States or an aerobics instructor. Let people know that while you can't fully understand their personal situation, you can try to understand how they feel.

6. **Listen with your whole body:** Maintain appropriate eye contact, lean slightly forward to show interest and attentiveness, nod your head occasionally or offer encouragement to confirm your continued interest. Listen with your whole body. (Remember the tips I shared in Sections II and III.)

7. **Eliminate listening tics:** Refrain from biting your lips, playing with your hair, glancing away at something else that interests you, checking your watch or looking at a clock, blowing your nose, turning away momentarily from the speaker, playing with jewelry or jingling the loose change in your pockets, and so on.

8. **Interrupt diplomatically:** Sometimes you just have to interrupt long-winded people. It may seem impolite, but the alternative is listening to a lengthy conversation. Try para-phrasing what the speaker just said, ask clarifying questions or tactfully end the conversation.

9. **Take notes but not copious notes:** During business conversations, serious discussions, customer complaint calls, on-the-job training instructions, it's okay to take notes. Don't hesitate to pull out a note pad or palm pilot. Say something like: "I want to be sure to capture this information," or "I want to be sure to remember this," or "That's such a neat statement, I don't want to forget it." Trying to take copious notes prevents the eye contact you need to assess the speaker's body language, voice inflection, vocal tone, pauses, pronunciation, accent and grammar. Take periodic notes. Capture essential information without distracting the speaker.

10. **Avoid biased listening insomuch as your prudence and principles allow:** Because we have opinions about certain types of people, we tend to be biased as to what they

might say. We may label any information they share as unimportant, irrelevant, negative, boring, unpleasant or even worthless. Biases are perceptual filters which distort what we see, hear and feel. They take us out of the context of the present situation and clutter what we hear with what we think we hear. We attach meanings to words, gestures and content that may create unnecessary interpersonal barriers.

11. **Listen empathetically:** Listen to the underlying meanings associated with what is being said. Empathy helps build trust and rapport. It eases the other person's emotional burden. People will open up to you once they feel you aren't being critical or judgmental. Empathizing doesn't mean you agree with the person's views. It means you understand their feelings and concerns

12. **Ask clarifying questions:** Timing is important. Hold your questions until you're sure the person can field questions unemotionally. That's the ideal timing. You may have to ask a question in the middle of someone's emotional outburst to calm them down. Ask clarifying questions, not judgmental questions. If people think you're being critical they'll stop talking to you. (If you want to end conversations, be critical and judgmental.) As a rule, ask questions, give comments and explanations, and share observations *after*, not before, someone's emotional release.

13. **Listen between the lines:** Sometimes the most revealing – and important – part of a conversation is what is *not* said or purposefully concealed. Why did the talker conceal details? Why did she divert her eyes and lower them when she said that? Why was he so evasive about what derailed his project? Why did the group seem uptight whenever he spoke? Why does she shield her mouth when she talks.

14. **Back-peddle from sugar-coated compliments:** How many times have you heard someone say, "We're cut from the same mold," or "We're so much alike," or "Hey,

good buddy," or "You're so special," or "You're the only one who understands me"? Expressions like these are manipulative and self-serving. The persuader is soliciting your support by assuming you share his or her philosophies, biases and ethics. When someone uses these ploys, listen between the lines to make sure you aren't being pulled into something you'll regret.

15. **Listen to yourself:** Become aware of your own listening ability. When are you at your empathetic best? What are your strong points? Do you interrupt people too often? Are you long-winded or short on patience? When are you most anxious or defensive? How well do you handle pauses and interruptions?

16. **Don't fake listening:** Give the talker your full time and attention, otherwise your disinterest or boredom will leak into your facial expressions and body language, your tone of voice, and the way you respond to breaks and pauses in the conversation. If you are unable to listen attentively, tactfully arrange a time when you can give your complete and undivided attention to the matter.

17. **Don't play hide and seek:** Some people listen because they do not want to disclose anything about themselves. They withhold their views, values, feelings, interests and personal biases for fear of public disapproval, criticism or embarrassment. This self-censorship is a way of avoiding responsibility in assuring a good communication experience. It takes two to communicate.

18. **Avoid mercenary listening:** Some people listen to embarrass or humiliate the speaker. They look for vulnerabilities in the speaker's conversational ability. They call attention to mispronounced words, or criticize someone's accent. They enter conversations on an ego trip and use them as platforms to tote their intellectual or experiential superiority. Their intent is to dismantle the speaker. The best way to defuse a mercenary's tactics is to use firm diplomacy. Say something

like, "That's the second (third or fourth) time you've criticized something I've said. I find your comments distracting (hurtful, offensive). I'd appreciate your not interrupting me at every turn. Perhaps we should postpone our conversation until you're in a better frame of mind." Mercenaries understand confrontational language. Be tactful, but firm; empathetic, but assertive.

19. Listening is revealing: When you listen attentively to others, you run the risk of hearing conflicting beliefs and values. Sometimes a particularly charismatic or persuasive person can rock your view of the world or rattle your self-concept. Being open-minded is the key, particularly when you hear new or controversial information.

20. Summarize important take-aways: Lawyers summarize their legal defenses. Speakers summarize the key points in their speeches. Writers include summary paragraphs in their books. Parents ask children to repeat instructions. Sales people close the sale. Summations are important. They provide a final opportunity to clarify important parts of the message to ensure that everyone is in agreement.

All of the "hearing aids" listed above will help you become an effective listener. What you have learned in this chapter is only a beginning. How well you develop your "hearing antennae" depends on your commitment, patience and enthusiasm. One thing is for certain, you can't talk and learn at the same time, but you can listen and learn every time. Use what you've learned in this chapter to help you hear the sounds of success.

> *Conversation...is a competitive exercise in which the first person to draw a breath is declared the listener.*
> *(Nathan Miller)*

VOICE OVERS

A Summary of Points to Remember

1. Hearing involves the physiological reception of sound, while listening applies to the perception of meaningful sound.
2. The audible you is just as important as the vocal, verbal and visible you.
3. You can become a better listener if you want to become a better listener, and you will become a better speaker when you practice listening.
4. Give people a good listening-to.
5. We learn very early in life that talking is rewarded more than listening.
6. Good listening is everyone's business, and good business is listening to everyone.
7. Listen with your whole body.

CHAPTER FIFTEEN
YOUR AWESOME NATURAL VOICE

Don't stand shivering upon the bank; plunge in at once and have it.
(Thomas Haliburton)

Is there such a thing as the perfect voice? Yes and no! An awful lot of people have come close to it. Their voices may not be perfect, but they have developed extraordinary natural voices. They have evolved into their voices by working on their vocal awareness and competence each and every day. They are masters of voice control. People like James Earl Jones, Walter Cronkite, Kathleen Sullivan, Julie Andrews, Ronald Reagan, Katie Couric, Peter Jennings, Diane Sawyer, Harry Reasoner, Dan Rather, Jane Pauley and Elizabeth Dole have built fantastic business images because they have developed awesome voices.

The broadcast media spend tens of millions of dollars searching for the perfect voice. Is their search over? Yes and no, again. Yes, they have an idea of what constitutes the perfect voice. And, no, they continue to fine tune what they believe to be the perfect verbal, vocal and visual image. What have they found? They believe the ideal voice must show controlled emotion, be lower pitched, moderately paced and have a model English accent. It must be free from "verbal hiccups" (my term) and free from other distracting qualities. It must be clear, smooth and project a moderately resonated volume. That's it! According to the people who have invested the most, earned the most and have the most to lose if they don't produce the "perfect voice." The qualities named above define the *voice that means business, makes business and keeps business.*

Before you throw your hands up in despair and say, "I'll never sound like James Earl Jones, Katie Couric, or Walter Cronkite," remember these words: "You can come close." I'm not kidding. I wouldn't be in this business if I thought otherwise. Each of the elements of the "perfect" voice is within your control. You may not have the resources, time or inclination to attain a Cronkite voice or a Couric voice, but you can find *your own awesome natural* voice.

As you've already become aware, the vocal advice and exercises contained in this book can help you add just the right amount of emotion when you speak. You'll be able to turn your volume up or down; increase your speaking rate at will and pace yourself; and change the tone and pitch of your voice to speak confidently anywhere and anytime.

> *Speech is power; speech is to persuade, to convert, to compel. (Ralph Waldo Emerson)*

BREAKING THE SOUND BARRIER

You may have spent twenty, thirty or forty years or more without giving a single thought to improving your vocal, verbal and visual image – but it's not too late. If you'll spend twenty, thirty or forty *minutes* or more each day to develop your natural voice, you'll understand what I mean when I say, "When you change your voice, you'll change your life."

Actually, you've already changed your voice which has changed your life. Between the ages of ten to fifteen, our voices change from boys' and girls' voices to men's and women's voices. I believe fifty percent of us retain our child's voice as we mature instead of developing our natural adult voice. It happens to all of us. People who have adult voices have worked at having adult voices, and they have *found* their adult voices because they have *found* themselves. As I've said before, your voice comes from somewhere, and that somewhere is called the real you. In a very real sense the *vocal you* either expresses or hides the *real you.* In vocal communication terms there are four main vocal qualities that will help you "break the sound barrier."

Let's take a quick look at those qualities now. They are: volume, pitch, tone and pace. Before you read further I want to remind you that your *natural* voice is the *perfect* voice for you. You don't have to sound – nor am I promising that you will sound – like Walter or Katie or James Earl. So, don't go vocally schizophrenic on me thinking someone or something can *steal* your true voice. Only you can do that. So, don't run from your true voice – learn to express it anywhere, anytime.

Studies have consistently shown that moderate volume range reflects confidence, poise, self-assurance, credibility and believability. Your natural volume may be a little higher or lower than Dan Rather's or Diane Sawyer's well-financed voices, but it will be at the right volume for you and in the right range for you to speak authoritatively and effectively.

When professional speakers tell me they are losing their voice, I ask to see their presentation, because the problem actually may have very little to do with voice. At a recent National Speakers Association (NSA) Convention, a well-known keynote speaker pulled me out of the breakout session we were both attending. In the hall, he said, "I hear you're the best voice coach in NSA. Well, I need help with my voice – I can't last through my presentations anymore."

I had attended his speech just a few hours earlier and had been very impressed with his power and ability to communicate. However, I had also noticed that he was spending long periods of time bent over the overhead projector he used onstage. His posture was affecting his ability to breathe properly and project his voice correctly.

The convention was almost over and I was scheduled to leave the next day, but he arranged to meet with me in the morning over breakfast. I had him practice some diaphragmatic breathing and posture exercises. I also suggested he raise the level of the overhead projector so he could change his slides and still stand relatively upright. And I told him, "Drink water! All speakers should drink at least three glasses of water an hour before they go on. You should also have a glass at your side so you can sip water throughout your presentation." He thanked me, gave me a check and we both left for our respective planes.

Three weeks later I got a letter from him saying, "Linda, at our breakfast you gave me three specific things to do and they've all worked. It's 5:30 p.m. and I just finished a full-day seminar. I'm happy to report my voice is as strong now after speaking for eight hours as it was early this morning." He also paid me the compliment of including another check, declaring, "The advice you gave me was worth twice what you charged me!"

Determinng the pitch of your natural voice involves recognizing whether it's high, low, thin, tense or throaty. Your natural voice will generally be more moderately pitched, but able to vary the pitch depending on the type of message being communicated. Your natural voice will have a pitch richness all its own.

Good tonality is the resonate vibrancy of your voice. It adds to the fullness and richness of your vocal quality. It lowers your voice and deepens your overall tone. You do not want to try to lower your voice artificially or force an unnatural low-pitched voice. That will place too much strain on your throat and vocal cords. Resonate voices are natural voices. Review the vocal aerobics exercises for volume and tonality in Chapter Eleven.

Pace, as you know, refers to the speed at which you speak. Most Americans speak at the rate of 120 to 160 with slight variations. Franklin D. Roosevelt spoke at 110 to 120 words per minute; John F. Kennedy spoke from 120 to 160, with gusts up to 180; Peter Jennings and Katie Couric chime in at 110 to 140. President George W. Bush speaks consistently at 90 - 110, with frequent pauses. Martin Luther King opened his "I Have a Dream" speech at 92 to 95 words per minute and finished at a rate of 140 to 155. Many good speakers vary the rate of speech depending on the mood they want to set, the composition of the audience, the nature of the occasion and the impact they want to make on the audience – whether it's an audience of one or a thousand.

Your natural speaking rate should be somewhat faster than normal to be seen as competent and persuasive. However, you should slow your speaking rate when you need to explain difficult or complex information. The key is to vary your rate to get your message across so that listeners want to hear what you have to say.

Well-placed pauses are effective pace regulators. They give you a chance to collect your thoughts and other people an opportunity to speak. Breaks in delivery can add drama to your message and keep it animated and interesting. Let's pause right now and spend a little time on the "pause that refreshes."

> *Speech is the index of the mind.*
> *(Seneca)*

THE PAUSE THAT REFRESHES

The pause is an incredibly powerful vocal tool which accents your spoken image and helps give you the authority, confidence and credibility you deserve. Pauses are excellent vocal devices – when they are used effectively – to give you time to relax, breathe and re-energize your voice. They help drive home an important point and dramatize your message.

Effective pauses demonstrate that you are comfortable with a few "syllables of silence" and that you feel confident and in control. Although it can be one of your most powerful vocal tools, lengthy pauses or filling in pauses can ruin an otherwise effective discussion, report or speech.

I worked with a telecommunications Vice-President who *padded* his pauses. He used fillers like "uh", or "er" and "you know" to cover the silence. (See Chapter 13.) Instead of allowing silent pauses to punctuate his message he inserted "verbal hiccups" which were distracting and embarrassing. When we eliminated his "hiccups," his message became much more attention-getting instead of attention-defeating.

One of my favorite stories about violin virtuoso, Isaac Stern, illustrates the power of the "pause that refreshes." He was once asked why some professional musicians sounded mechanical and others, playing the same musical score, sounded artistic. He replied, "The important thing is not the notes. It's the intervals between the notes." The same concept applies whenever you speak. The important thing is not *your words, but the intervals (pauses) between your words.*

Learn how to shape your message with strategically-placed pauses. The difference in your delivery will be well worth the time and effort. I would be remiss if I failed to stress that learning to pause effectively is more difficult than it seems. I can think of many well-known professional speakers, TV and news personalities and professional trainers (I won't name them because I don't want to embarrass them) who speak well, but are not considered as especially dynamic presenters. They speak without pauses in an endless ribbon of verbage that gets tiresome.

One of the best strategies you can use to heighten the dramatic effect of your message is to craft pauses into the flow of your presentations. The same thing applies to one-on-one conversations or group discussions. Pauses that refresh are pauses that can enliven, enlighten and energize any meeting, interview or sales call.

Immediate Benefits of Silent Pauses

1. Pauses add a sense of authority and control to your messages, conversations and presentations.
2. Effective pauses call attention to the importance of the words just spoken.
3. Pauses punctuate the pace of your delivery and let the person you're talking to know when you've come to the end of a thought.
4. Pauses demonstrate you are comfortable with silence and use silence to dramatize important transitions and key points.
5. Carefully planned pauses allow you to catch your breath so you can stay in your natural voice.
6. Pauses give people a chance to absorb and appreciate what you say.
7. Pauses add dramatics and theatrics to excite listeners.
8. Pauses can help control inattentive or disruptive people by calling attention to them.

> *Pauses give your (message) the design you would find in a good poem or essay. Just as the written page has structure, headlines, margins, bold print, bullets and spaces, spoken words need the contrast of silence and sound for beautiful design. (Natalie Rogers, psychotherapist and former actress)*

HOW I FOUND MY NATURAL VOICE AND MY CAREER

Once upon a time I was Public Relations Director of the Cleveland Hearing and Speech Center. I also had a regular speech-communication spot on WJKW-TV8's noontime show. Life was good. I was at the top of my profession as a speech pathologist, dating the anchorman for the Evening News and auditioning for a show called *PM Magazine.* Not bad for a formerly shy only child from Detroit, Michigan. I enjoyed the TV spotlight and was not ashamed of being bitten by the showbiz bug.

I had written a perfect three-minute piece on autograph collecting for the *PM Magazine* spot. Every word was carefully crafted – and memorized. I contracted a cosmetologist, hired a professional image consultant and bought the prefect business attire. I wanted to look good, feel good and sound good. As a seasoned professional, I knew that all of my preparation would pay off. I was confident. I had connections and I had moxie. Family and colleagues said I had been groomed for this spot. "It's a slam dunk," they said. "You're a natural. The job was made for you."

Now you're probably thinking by now that I aced the audition. Believe it or not, I bombed. I was crushed. "It was a speaking part," I reminded myself. "I'm a speech communications professional. It's what I do for a living. How could

I have failed to impress them with my consummate communication skills?" I gave myself time for a good cry and then made another appointment with the show's producer and director. Have you ever heard the expression, "If you don't want to know, don't ask"? Well...I asked, and the answer I received changed my life forever.

The director replayed the tape of my presentation. Then he said, "Linda, if you had auditioned for Romper Room, you would have had every agent in America wanting to represent you."

I cracked a suspicious smile. And then I said, "Thanks, but I think I hear a *but* tucked away in that compliment."

He nodded. Then he said something I've never forgotten: "Linda, you've got the most pedagogic voice I have ever heard. If you want to make it in this business, you're going to have to get a new voice."

I remember my lower jaw dropping into my lap. Before I could regain my composure, he continued: "You're a bright, beautiful, articulate woman, but you sound like a little girl."

I was stunned! I still don't remember how I made it back to the speech center. But I remember how shaken I was. And I remember the confused look on my solemn twin's face in the car mirror. I remember my embarrassment and smudging my mascara. But I also remember a new woman was born that day. I resolved that very afternoon to find the perfect voice – my perfect voice – so I'd never have to apologize for the way I sound again.

I have since come to realize that my audition wasn't for the *PM Magazine*. I was auditioning for a career as a voice coach. I didn't know it at the time, of course, but I was being "knighted" as a voice coach.

I have spent years developing my vocal, verbal and visual image. I have travelled the same path as Demosthenes, Patrick Henry, Martin Luther King and scores of other great orators. That path is the same one you must travel to find your true voice – your awesome natural voice. It is the path that leads through the sound barrier. It is the path marked "how to speak with athority."

You've taken an important step on that path by purchasing this book. Your true voice, your natural voice may be just a page away, a practice exercise away, a breath away. I have shared my story with you to encourage you to move past your own disappointments, insecurities and fears. If I can do it, you can do it! I mean that. My sincere hope is that sometime in the very near future, you will be able to look in the mirror, smile and say, in your own natural voice, "I've found you and you sound awesome."

> *The magic of the tongue is the most dangerous of all spells. (Edward G. E. Buliver-Lytton)*

VOICE OVERS

A Summary of Points to Remember

1. We evolve into our natural voices by faithfully working on our vocal and verbal awareness every day.
2. The ideal voice must show controlled emotion, be lower-pitched, moderately paced, have a model English accent, and be free from distracting qualities.
3. When you change your voice, you'll change your life.
4. Most people never find their "adult" voice.
5. In vocal communication terms, there are four main vocal qualities which can help you break the sound barrier: pitch, resonance, volume and pace.
6. Your natural voice is the perfect voice for you.
7. Studies have consistently shown that moderate volume range reflects confidence, poise, self-assurance, credibility and believability.
8. Well-placed pauses are effective pace regulators.
9. Effective pauses demonstrate how comfortable you are with a few "syllables of silence."
10. Just as important as the words you use are the spaces between the words.

BIBLIOGRAPHY

Allen, Steve, *How to Make a Speech*, New York, McGraw-Hill, 1986.

Birdwhistell, Ray, *Kinesics and Context*, Philadelphia, Univ. of Penn. 1970.

Bombeck, Erma, *If Life is a Bowl of Cherries, What Am I Doing in the Pits?* New York, McGraw-Hill, 1978.

Byrum-Gau, Beverly, *It Depends*, Sherman Oaks, CA, Alfred Pub. Co. 1981.

Cundiff, Merlyn, *Kinesics: The Power of Silent Command*, West Nyack, NY, Parker Pub. 1972.

Dimitrius, Jo-Ellen, *Put Your Best Foot Forward*, New York, Scribner, 2000.

Gschwandtner, Gerhard, *Nonverbal Selling Power*, Englewood Cliffs, NJ, Prentice Hall, 1985.

Johnston, Joni, *Appearance Obsession: Learning to Love the Way You Look*, Deerfield Beach, FL, 1994.

King, Larry, *How to Talk to Anyone, Anytime, Anywhere*, New York, Crown Pub., 1994.

McMahon, Ed., *The Art of Public Speaking*, New York, Putnam, 1986.

Partnow, Elaine, *The Quotable Woman*, New York, Facts on File, Inc., 1982.

Mehrabian, Albert, *Nonverbal Communication*, Chicago, Aldine, 1972.

Rogers, Natalie, *Talk Power*, Sterling, VA, Capital Books, 1999.

Vassallo, Wanda, *Speaking With Confidence*, Cincinnati, 1990.

Whiteside, Robert, *Face Language*, New York, Frederick Fell Publishing, 1974.

York, Brenda, "Design Your Image of Success," PSP, Oct. 1983.

Zunin, Leonard and Natalie Zunin, *Contact: The First Four Minutes*, New York, Ballantine Books, 1972.

ABOUT THE AUTHOR

Linda Shields is a nationally-recognized voice coach, speech pathologist, and the president of Speaking With Authority Inc. Described as "electric" on and off the stage, she is recognized as one of the National Speakers Association's best presenters and vocal coaches. She is a frequent guest speaker at the association's conventions and conferences.

She holds a Master of Science degree in Speech Pathology from the University of Michigan (Ann Arbor) and a Certificate of Clinical Competence in Speech and Language Pathology from the American Speech and Hearing Association. She is certified by the North Carolina Board of Examiners for Speech-Language Pathology, and for many years she taught speech, voice and drama at all educational levels.

Linda makes frequent TV appearances and is a regular guest on radio programs. Her client list reads like a "Who's Who" of the entertainment, media and professional presenters' worlds. Her prestigious client list includes: ABC Broadcasting Company, CNN, Nortel, Sprint, U.S.O. Germany, Century 21 Realty, Grand Ole Opry, and the U.S. Government.

She is also a national fitness presenter and master trainer with Interactive Fitness Trainers of America (IFTA).

On a personal note, Linda is an avid reader, enthusiastic traveler, and her son and daughter-in-law, Todd and Ginny's biggest fan.